TEACHER RECOMMENDED

10th GRADE NEXT GENERATION LEARNING STANDARDS

ELA ENGLISH LANGUAGE ARTS

TOPICS COVERED

- CONTEXT CLUE ANALYSIS
- SAT/ACT TEST STRATEGIES
- AUTHOR'S PURPOSE IDENTIFICATION
- ACADEMIC VOCABULARY BUILDING
- ETYMOLOGY & WORD PARTS
- CONNOTATION VS DENOTATION
- RHETORICAL STRATEGY ANALYSIS
- WORD RELATIONSHIP PATTERNS
- TECHNICAL VOCABULARY MASTERY
- INFERENCE SKILL DEVELOPMENT

ArgoPrep is one of the leading providers of supplemental educational products ,and services. We offer affordable and effective test prep solutions to educators, parents and students. Learning should be fun and easy! To access more resources, visit us at www.argoprep.com.

Our goal is to make your life easier, so let us know how we can help you by emailing us at info@argoprep.com.

- ArgoPrep is a recipient of the prestigious **Mom's Choice Award**.
- ArgoPrep also received the 2019 **Seal of Approval** from Homeschool.com for our award-winning workbooks.
- ArgoPrep was awarded the 2019 **National Parenting Products Award**, **Gold Medal Parent's Choice Award** and **the Tillywig Brain Child Award.**

ISBN: 978-1962936293

Published by Argo Brothers.

Table of Contents

WEEK 1

Advanced Vocabulary Development

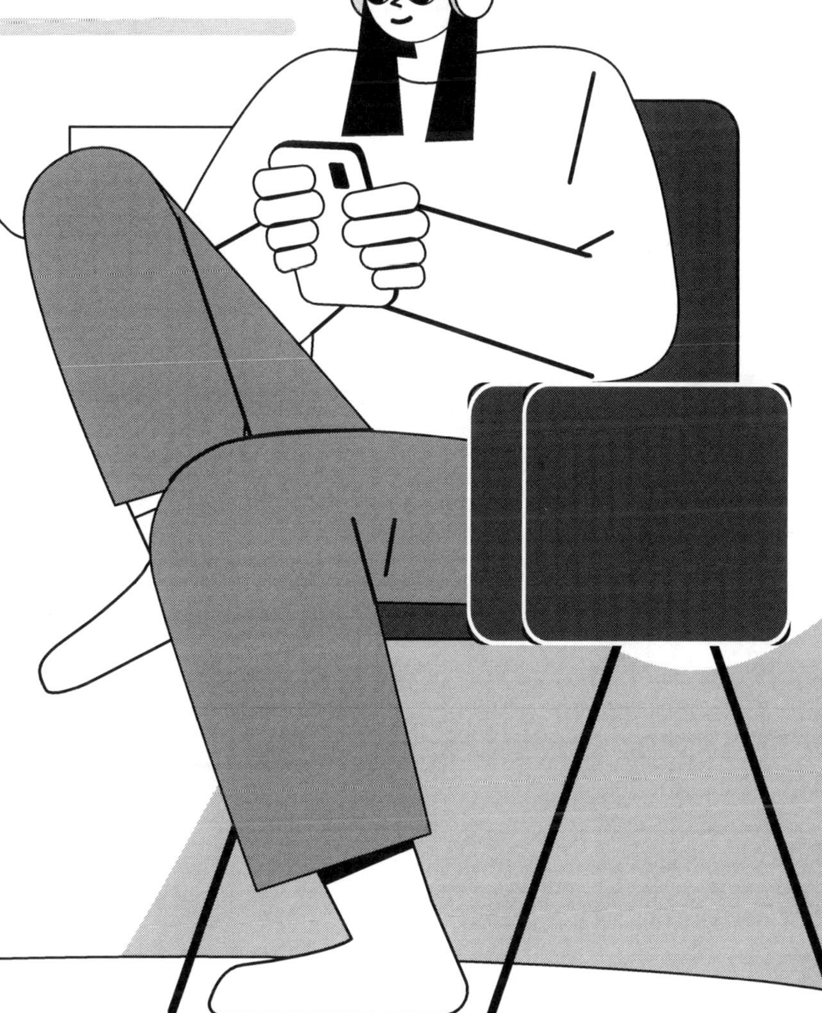

Learn strategies to understand challenging vocabulary using context clues, etymology, and word roots. Explore denotation vs. connotation and how word choice reveals meaning and author intent.

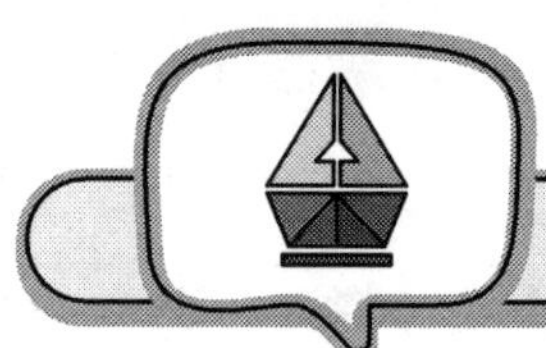

Introduction

Welcome to Week 1 of your 10th grade journey! This week, you'll develop sophisticated word analysis strategies essential for tackling complex texts across subjects. By mastering context clues, etymological analysis, and connotative meaning, you'll dramatically expand your vocabulary and improve your reading comprehension. These skills will help you navigate challenging literature, scientific articles, and standardized tests with greater confidence and precision.

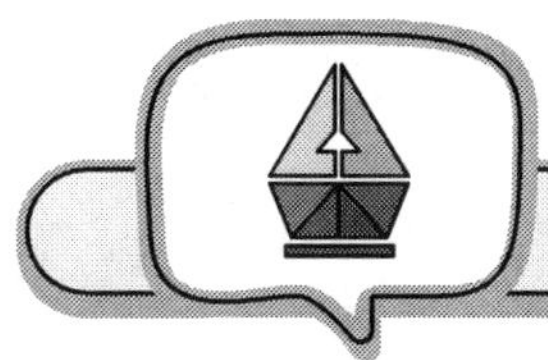

Day 1

Week 1 • Advanced Vocabulary Development

Using Context for Advanced Vocabulary

Today, you'll learn how to use context clues to figure out unfamiliar words in complex texts. This skill is especially important when reading challenging literature or technical writing, where you can't always stop to look up every word.

By the end of this lesson, you'll be able to:

- Identify different types of context clues in challenging texts.
- Use surrounding information to determine word meanings.
- Apply context analysis strategies when reading complex material.
- Recognize when context provides partial or multiple possible meanings.

Key Concept #1: Types of Advanced Context Clues

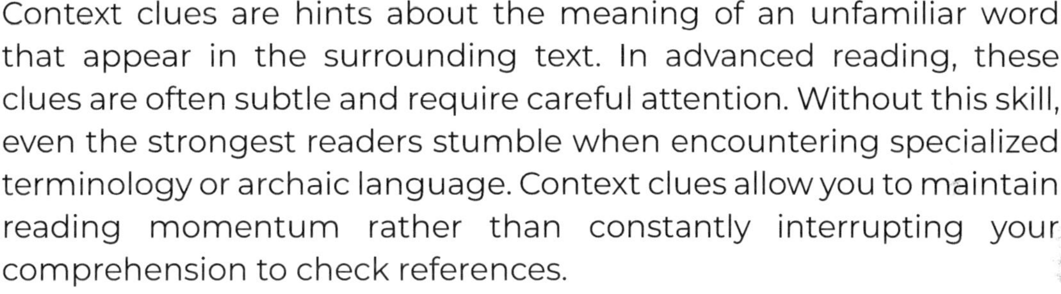

Context clues are hints about the meaning of an unfamiliar word that appear in the surrounding text. In advanced reading, these clues are often subtle and require careful attention. Without this skill, even the strongest readers stumble when encountering specialized terminology or archaic language. Context clues allow you to maintain reading momentum rather than constantly interrupting your comprehension to check references.

Why It Matters

When you're reading complex texts—whether it's a scientific article, a classic novel, or a historical document—you'll constantly run into unfamiliar words. Being able to figure out meanings from context keeps you from interrupting your reading flow every few sentences to check a dictionary. More importantly, context often reveals specific meanings that dictionaries might miss, especially for:

- Words with multiple definitions
- Technical or specialized terminology
- Archaic language in historical texts
- Culturally specific terms
- Words used in unusual or creative ways

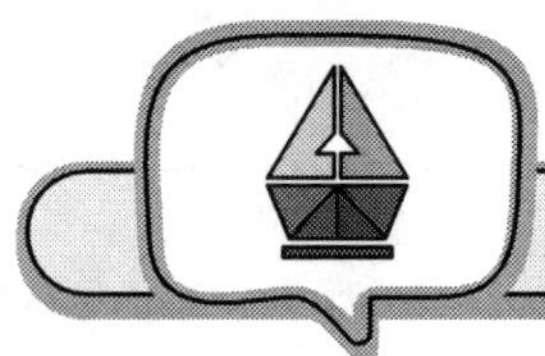

Week 1 • Advanced Vocabulary Development

Mastering this skill helps you:

- Approach challenging texts with greater confidence.
- Develop reading independence when dictionaries aren't available.
- Recognize how words function differently across disciplines.
- Build vocabulary more efficiently through natural exposure.

Primary Types of Context Clues

Definition clues directly explain what a word means.

- "The platypus, a monotreme that lays eggs despite being a mammal, defies traditional classification."
- "His mendacity—his habit of telling deliberate lies—eventually cost him every friendship."

Synonym clues offer words with similar meanings nearby.

- "The arboreal creatures, those tree-dwelling mammals, were rarely seen on the ground."
- "Her loquacious nature was obvious; she talked constantly and rarely gave others a chance to speak."

Antonym clues provide opposite meanings.

- "Unlike his garrulous brother, Nev was reticent and spoke only when necessary."
- "While some workers were diligent, others were indolent and accomplished little during their shifts."

Example clues illustrate the concept.

- "They discussed various phobias: fear of heights, fear of enclosed spaces, and fear of spiders."
- "The symphony contained multiple crescendos, moments where the music swelled dramatically in volume."

Inference clues require piecing together multiple hints.

- "After three sleepless nights preparing her case, Maya's arguments before the judge were cogent and persuasive, earning her a favorable ruling."
- "The spelunker's lamp flickered as he ventured deeper into the winding underground passages, revealing stalactites that hung like stone icicles from the cavern ceiling."

Example 1: Analyzing Definition Clues

"The monarch's increasing prerogative—his exclusive right to exercise authority—alarmed Parliament, which feared the dissolution of traditional governance structures. Though such executive powers had historical precedent, their expansion threatened to unbalance the delicate equilibrium between Crown and Commons."

In this example, the formal definition appears as an appositive phrase that directly explains "prerogative" as "his exclusive right to exercise authority."

The dash signals this straightforward definition and helps readers immediately understand this crucial political concept.

Example 2: Recognizing Example Clues

"Mei's xenophobia manifested in countless ways throughout her first semester abroad. She refused invitations to local celebrations, insisted on eating only familiar foods from home, and visibly tensed whenever her roommates spoke in their native tongue rather than English. Only after joining a cultural exchange program did her fear of unfamiliar customs begin to diminish."

Here, the meaning of "xenophobia" isn't directly stated but is illustrated through specific behaviors that demonstrate fear of foreign elements.

The examples provide an indirect definition through illustration rather than an explicit statement.

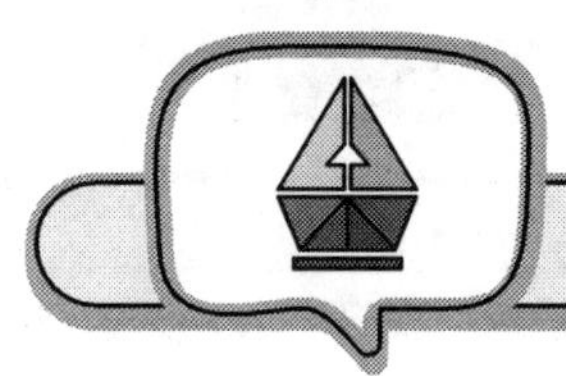

Week 1 • Practice Activity 1

Context Clue Classification

Directions: For each bolded word, write a short definition and identify the type of context clue provided.

The ancient manuscript revealed the **esoteric** practices of the civilization—religious rituals intended only for initiated members and kept hidden from ordinary citizens. Unlike the **ubiquitous** pottery artifacts found throughout the region, these texts were exceedingly rare, discovered only in the private chambers of high priests. The archaeologists approached the scrolls with great **trepidation**; their excitement about the discovery was tempered by fear of damaging the fragile documents. Despite their careful handling, several sections had already deteriorated beyond recognition, **obscuring** critical information and making certain passages impossible to read.

1. esoteric

Definition: ....

Type of context clue: ....

2. ubiquitous

Definition: ....

Type of context clue: ....

3. trepidation

Definition: ....

Type of context clue: ....

4. obscuring

Definition: ....

Type of context clue: ....

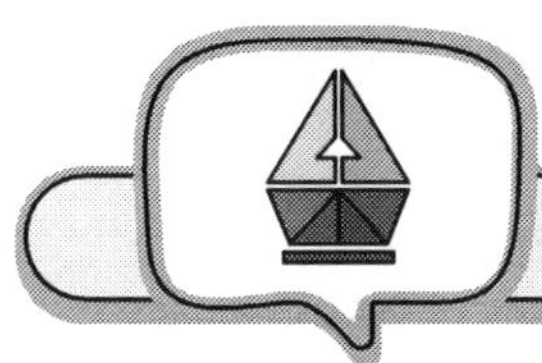

Key Concept #2: Context Analysis Strategies

Why It Matters

Strategic context analysis transforms vocabulary building from random memorization to methodical deduction. This approach treats unfamiliar words as puzzles to solve rather than obstacles to comprehension, developing critical thinking skills that transfer across all academic disciplines.

Mastering this skill helps you:

- Maintain reading momentum without constant interruptions.
- Determine the meaning when dictionary definitions are inadequate.
- Recognize specialized meanings within particular fields.
- Build vocabulary more organically through active engagement.

The Context Analysis Process

When using context to determine meaning, follow these steps:

1. Identify the unknown word and note its part of speech.
2. Look for direct definition clues in the same sentence.
3. Search for examples, synonyms, or contrasts nearby.
4. Consider the overall topic and tone of the passage.
5. Combine all contextual evidence to form a possible definition.
6. Test your definition by substituting it in the original sentence.

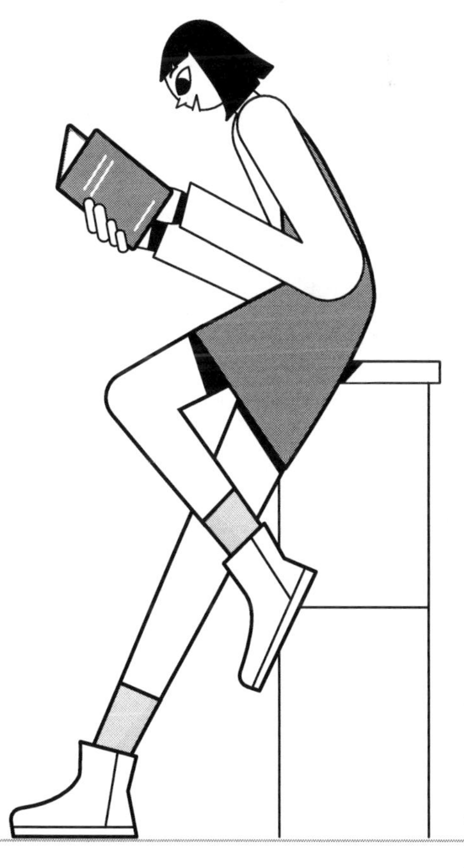

Example 3: Context Analysis

"The erudite professor captivated her students with lectures that seamlessly connected historical events to contemporary issues. Unlike her colleagues, who relied heavily on textbooks, she drew from decades of independent research and personal interviews with primary sources. Students often found themselves taking detailed notes, hoping to absorb not just facts but her sophisticated analytical approach that reflected years of scholarly dedication."

To determine the meaning of "erudite":

1. Note that it describes a professor (suggesting an academic quality).
2. Observe that the professor gives captivating lectures connecting complex topics.
3. Recognize the contrast with colleagues (suggesting superiority in some aspect).
4. Note references to "independent research" and "sophisticated analytical approach."
5. Identify connections to "scholarly dedication."

From these contextual elements, we can determine that "erudite" means "possessing or showing great knowledge gained from study and reading."

Context Analysis Application

Directions: Read the excerpt below and answer the questions that follow.

Excerpt from "The Tale of Genji" by Murasaki Shikibu

Though the August Emperor had many consorts of unquestioned lineage, he was most drawn to the lady not from the highest rank. Her father was merely a governor of a distant province, yet her ineffable charm and gentle disposition captivated the Emperor beyond reason. The grand courtiers found this infatuation a source of great consternation and whispered that the lady possessed some supernatural allure.

The lady's apartments were modest compared to those of her rivals, yet when the Emperor visited, he found them more congenial than the ostentatious chambers of the senior consorts. These visits became so frequent that court officials grew apprehensive about neglected matters of state.

"His Majesty's partiality for the lady has become immoderate," lamented the Minister of the Right to his confidants. "Such capricious affections might destabilize the established order."

Indeed, the Emperor recognized the impropriety of his devotion, yet found himself powerless against his sentiments. When courtiers remonstrated indirectly about his frequent visits to her pavilion, he acknowledged their concerns but did not alter his behavior.

Question 1: What does the word "consort" most likely mean in this context?

- **A.** a female ruler with political authority
- **B.** a musician who plays at royal events
- **C.** a companion or spouse of a royal figure
- **D.** a servant who attends to the Emperor

Question 2: Based on the passage, what does "ineffable" most likely mean?

- **A.** loud and attention-seeking
- **B.** too great or beautiful to be described in words
- **C.** mysterious in an untrustworthy way
- **D.** faint and difficult to perceive

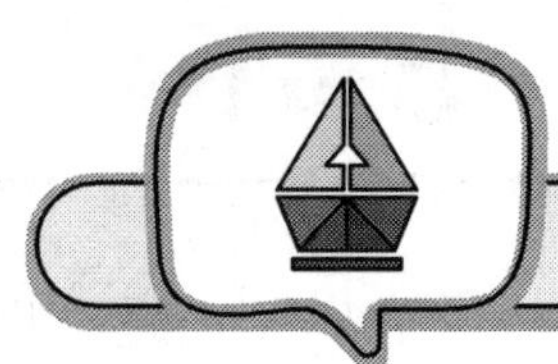

Week 1 • Practice Activity 2

Question 3: What does "ostentatious" suggest about the senior consorts' chambers?

A. They were simple and unadorned.

B. They were dark and unwelcoming.

C. They were designed for official business only.

D. They were luxurious to the point of showing off wealth or status.

Question 4: What does the word "remonstrated" most likely mean in the sentence:

"When courtiers remonstrated indirectly about his frequent visits to her pavilion, he acknowledged their concerns but did not alter his behavior."?

A. spoke up to express disapproval or objection

B. complimented or praised politely

C. made formal requests for financial support

D. ignored the situation completely

Note:

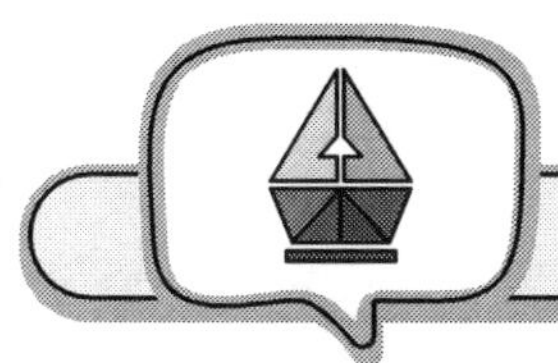

Week 1 • Practice Activity 3

Scientific Context Analysis

Directions: Read the excerpt about rainforest ecosystems and determine the meaning of each bolded term using context clues. Explain what clues helped you reach your conclusion.

The extraordinary biodiversity of Amazonian rainforests derives from multiple ecological factors operating simultaneously. Perhaps most significant is the **stratification** of the forest into discrete, vertical layers, each creating unique microclimates and specialized habitats. From the forest floor to the emergent canopy, these distinct zones support remarkably different communities of organisms.

Many species found in these forests are **endemic**, occurring nowhere else on Earth. These organisms have evolved in isolation, developing specialized adaptations to highly specific environmental conditions. Unfortunately, such specialization makes these species particularly vulnerable to habitat fragmentation caused by **anthropogenic** activities such as logging and agricultural expansion.

The cumulative impact of even small disturbances can trigger cascading effects throughout the ecosystem. For instance, the **extirpation** of certain keystone species—those having disproportionate influence relative to their abundance—can destabilize entire food webs. The loss of large predators provides a sobering example, as their removal often leads to population explosions among herbivores that subsequently decimate plant communities.

Question 1: In the sentence, "Perhaps most significant is the stratification of the forest into discrete vertical layers, each creating unique microclimates and specialized habitats," which context clue best helps the reader understand the meaning of stratification?

A. "unique microclimates" and "specialized habitats"

B. "discrete vertical layers"

C. "most significant" and "forest"

D. "support remarkably different communities"

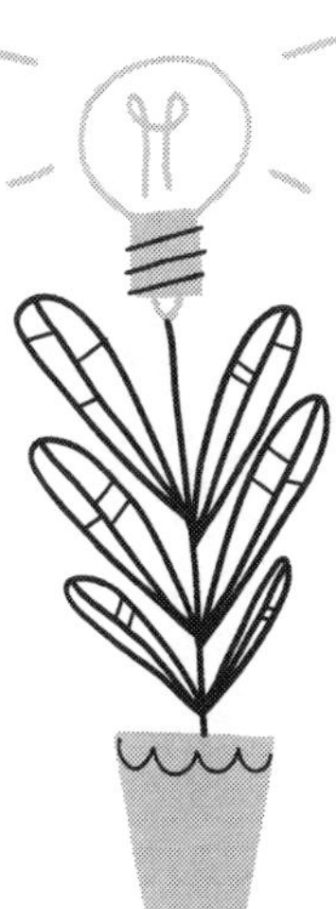

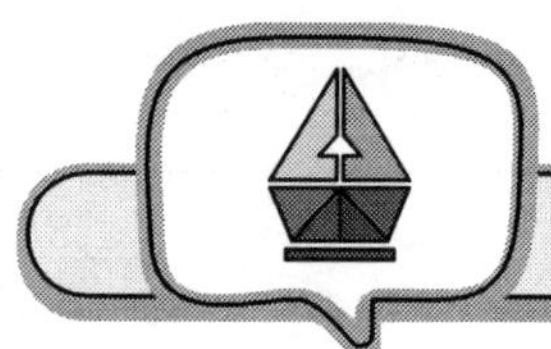

Week 1 • Practice Activity 3

Question 2: In the sentence, "such specialization makes these species particularly vulnerable to habitat fragmentation caused by anthropogenic activities such as logging and agricultural expansion," what context clues best help the reader determine the meaning of anthropogenic?

A. "habitat fragmentation" and "species"

B. "activities such as logging and agricultural expansion"

C. "specialization" and "environmental conditions"

D. "biodiversity" and "microclimates"

Question 3: What does stratification most likely mean as used in the passage?

A. the layering of different forest zones

B. the removal of trees from a forest

C. the spread of plant species across the forest

D. the migration of animals to new environments

Question 4: In the passage, what does endemic most likely mean?

A. rare and endangered

B. easily adaptable to many environments

C. common across all ecosystems

D. found only in one specific location

Question 5: What does extirpation most likely mean as used in the passage?

A. the increase in animal population

B. the protection of vulnerable species

C. the local extinction or removal of a species

D. the spread of disease among organisms

Great job! Tomorrow, we'll explore how word origins help us understand advanced vocabulary.

Building Word Knowledge Through Etymology

By the end of this lesson, you'll be able to:

- Identify Greek and Latin roots in advanced academic vocabulary.
- Use your knowledge of prefixes and suffixes to decode unfamiliar terms.
- Recognize patterns in word formation to expand your vocabulary.
- Apply etymological analysis to technical terminology across subject areas.

Key Concept #1: Word Roots as Meaning Keys

Why It Matters

Etymology—the study of word origins—provides a strategic approach to vocabulary that goes beyond memorization. Most advanced academic terms in English derive from Greek and Latin roots, making knowledge of these components invaluable for decoding complex vocabulary. Rather than memorizing hundreds of individual words, you can learn a smaller number of roots that unlock the meaning of thousands of terms.

Mastering this skill helps you:

- Decipher unfamiliar words in standardized tests and academic texts.
- Recognize relationships between seemingly unrelated terms.
- Remember vocabulary more effectively by understanding its components.
- Build your vocabulary exponentially by learning key roots.

Essential Latin and Greek Roots

When examining etymology, follow these steps to unlock word meanings:

1. Identify the root(s) at the core of the word.
2. Notice prefixes at the beginning that modify the meaning.
3. Recognize suffixes at the end that often indicate part of speech.
4. Combine these elements to understand the word's literal meaning.
5. Connect this etymology to the word's current usage.

Example 1: Analyzing Scientific Terminology

"Photosynthesis represents one of the most fundamental biochemical processes on Earth. This intricate sequence transforms light energy into chemical energy, enabling plants, algae, and certain bacteria to manufacture glucose from carbon dioxide and water. While sunlight provides the initial energy source, chlorophyll—the photoreceptive pigment in chloroplasts—is essential for capturing these light wavelengths and initiating the photochemical reactions."

Let's analyze these scientific terms through their Greek roots:

- **Photo/synthesis** = photo (light) + synthesis (putting together) → "putting together with light"
- **Bio/chemical** = bio (life) + chemical → "chemistry related to living things"
- **Chloro/phyll** = chloro (green) + phyll (leaf) → "green leaf pigment"
- **Photo/receptive** = photo (light) + receptive (receiving) → "receiving light"
- **Photo/chemical** = photo (light) + chemical → "chemistry involving light"

Understanding these Greek roots helps you recognize that all these terms relate to processes involving light and its interactions with living organisms.

Example 2: Analyzing Humanities Vocabulary

"The protagonist's metamorphosis from naive optimist to cynical realist reflected the author's own disillusionment with post-war society. Throughout the narrative, this psychological transformation manifests through increasingly misanthropic dialogue and introspective passages that reveal the character's changing philosophy."

Let's break down these terms through their Greek and Latin roots:

- **Prot/agon/ist** = proto (first) + agon (struggle) + ist (one who) → "one who struggles in the first role"
- **Meta/morph/osis** = meta (change) + morph (form) + osis (process) → "process of changing form"
- **Dis/illusion/ment** = dis (removal) + illusion + ment (state of) → "state of having illusions removed"
- **Psych/o/log/ical** = psyche (mind) + logos (study) + ical (relating to) → "relating to the study of the mind"
- **Mis/anthrop/ic** = mis (bad) + anthropos (human) + ic (relating to) → "relating to a dislike of humans"
- **Intro/spect/ive** = intro (inward) + spect (look) + ive (tending to) → "tending to look inward"
- **Phil/o/soph/**y = philo (love) + sophia (wisdom) + y (state or condition) → "love of wisdom"

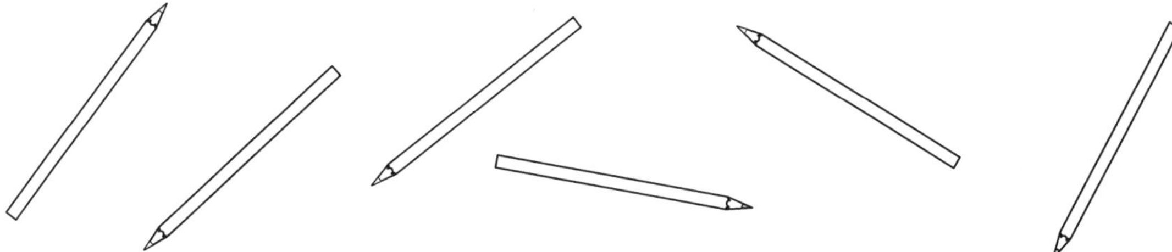

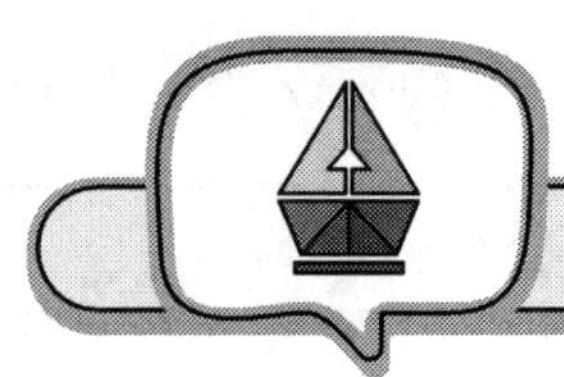

Week 1 • Practice Activity 1

Root Word Analysis

Directions: Break down each word into its roots and affixes. Then explain how these parts contribute to the word's meaning.

1. neuroscience

Break down the parts: ....

Explain the meaning: ....

2. telekinesis

Break down the parts: ....

Explain the meaning: ....

3. oligarchy

Break down the parts: ....

Explain the meaning: ....

4. retrospective

Break down the parts: ....

Explain the meaning: ....

5. malevolent

Break down the parts: ....

Explain the meaning: ....

6. philanthropy

Break down the parts: ....

Explain the meaning: ....

7. claustrophobia

Break down the parts: ....

Explain the meaning: ....

Key Concept #2: Prefixes and Suffixes as Meaning Modifiers

Why It Matters

Prefixes and suffixes transform root meanings in predictable ways, allowing you to understand subtle differences between related words. By learning these common affixes, you can decode complex terminology even when the root meanings aren't immediately obvious.

Mastering this skill helps you:

- Distinguish between related terms with important distinctions.
- Recognize negative, intensifying, or directional modifications to meaning.
- Understand how different parts of speech relate to the same word family.
- Develop greater precision in your own academic writing.

Power Prefixes and Significant Suffixes

To analyze how prefixes and suffixes modify meaning:

1. Identify the base word or root.
2. Determine how the prefix changes the root's direction, negates it, or otherwise modifies it.
3. Notice how the suffix indicates part of speech or adds meaning.
4. Recognize patterns of prefix and suffix usage across multiple words.
5. Apply this knowledge to unfamiliar words with familiar affixes.

Example 3: Analyzing Prefix Patterns

Consider how different prefixes modify the same root in these social science terms:

- **Con/form** = con (with) + form → to comply with existing standards
- **De/form** = de (away from) + form → to alter shape in a negative way
- **In/form** = in (into) + form → to put knowledge into someone
- **Re/form** = re (again) + form → to form again, to improve by change
- **Trans/form** = trans (across) + form → to change completely

Each prefix creates a distinct meaning from the same root "form," demonstrating how understanding these patterns can help you differentiate between related concepts.

Example 4: Analyzing Suffix Patterns

Notice how different suffixes create various parts of speech from the same root:

- Analyze (verb) = to examine methodically
- Analysis (noun) = the process of examining methodically
- Analyst (noun) = person who analyzes
- Analytic (adjective) = relating to analysis
- Analytically (adverb) = in an analytical manner

Understanding these suffix patterns helps you recognize how words function grammatically and how they relate to one another within word families.

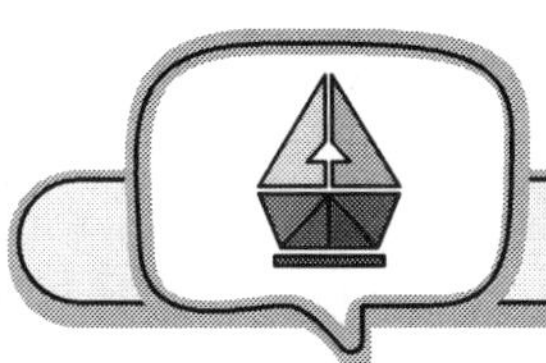

Word Family Exploration

Directions: Read the scientific article excerpt and answer the questions that follow.

Excerpt from "Neuroplasticity and Cognitive Development"

Neuroplasticity—the brain's remarkable capacity to reorganize neural pathways based on experience—fundamentally challenges earlier conceptions of neural development. Contemporary neuroscientists recognize that the brain remains malleable throughout the lifespan, continuously adapting to environmental stimuli through synaptogenesis and neural pruning. This neurological flexibility allows for significant cognitive adaptations even after critical developmental periods.

Research demonstrates that neurogenesis—the formation of new neurons—continues in specific brain regions throughout adulthood. However, neurodegeneration becomes increasingly prevalent with age, particularly in individuals with genetic predispositions to neurocognitive disorders. Environmental neurotoxins can further compromise neural integrity, accelerating cognitive decline.

Neuroscientific interventions often focus on neuroregeneration strategies that promote neural health and compensatory mechanisms. Through neuroimaging techniques, researchers can monitor neurochemical changes associated with these interventions, providing valuable insights into restorative neurotherapy approaches.

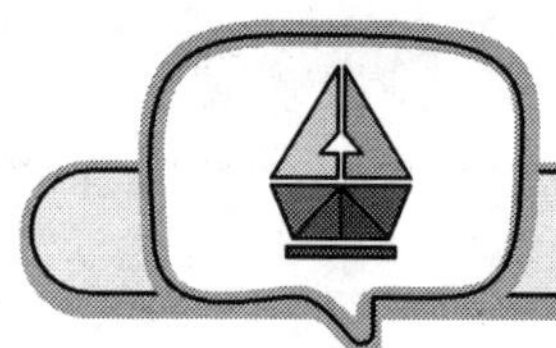

Week 1 • Practice Activity 2

Question 1: The words—neuroplasticity, neurogenesis, neurodegeneration, and neuroregeneration—share a common root. What does the root "neuro-" mean?

A. "Neuro" refers to the nervous system or brain.

B. "Neuro" means flexibility or growth.

C. "Neuro" is related to physical muscles and bones.

D. "Neuro" describes emotional responses.

Question 2: How does the prefix in neurodegeneration change the meaning of the root word?

A. It emphasizes flexibility in brain activity.

B. It refers to the growth of new brain cells.

C. It suggests a decline or breakdown of brain cells.

D. It indicates the root word is unrelated to the brain.

Question 3: What is the best definition of neuroplasticity based on the passage?

A. the brain becoming more rigid over time

B. the brain's ability to reorganize itself based on experience

C. the decline of brain cells due to aging

D. the loss of neurons from trauma or disease

Question 4: What does neurotoxins most likely mean in the context of the passage?

A. substances that enhance brain development

B. electrical signals used in brain imaging

C. proteins that improve neural communication

D. harmful chemicals that damage the nervous system

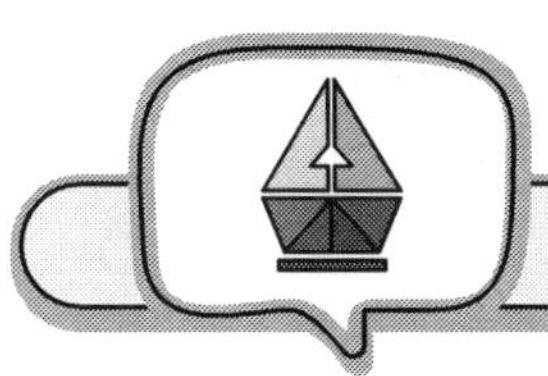

Week 1 • Practice Activity 3

Etymology in Context

Directions: Read the excerpt from this traditional folktale and determine how etymology helps clarify the meaning of each bolded word.

The village elder was renowned for his omniscience—the children believed he knew everything under the sun and beyond. When drought threatened the harvest, the villagers sought his circumspect advice, knowing his careful considerations would account for all possibilities. Though some young men advocated immediate action, the elder's response was unequivocal: they must wait for the polychronic signs that had guided their ancestors for generations.

"Our predecessors understood that nature communicates through multivocal patterns," he explained. "The antediluvian wisdom carved into the temple walls speaks of synchronicity between celestial movements and terrestrial needs."

The impatient youth found this approach antiquated, preferring contemporary solutions to supernatural intercession. Their vociferous objections echoed through the meeting hall. Yet the elder remained imperturbable, his equanimity a stark contrast to their agitation.

"Benevolence without wisdom becomes maleficence," he cautioned. "Our benefactors did not endow us with these traditions without purpose."

Question 1: How does understanding the etymology of omniscience help clarify its meaning in this passage?

A. The prefix omni- means "all," and the root -science means "knowledge," so omniscience means "all-knowing."

B. The word is derived from a Greek term for "vision," so it suggests the elder sees the future.

C. Omniscience refers to someone with limited knowledge of nature and ritual.

D. Omni- means "some," so omniscience describes someone with partial insight.

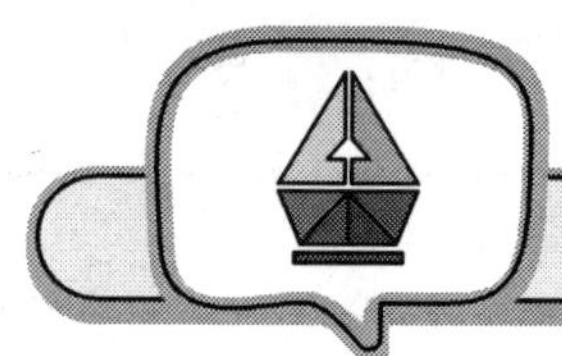

Week 1 • Practice Activity 3

Question 2: What does the word circumspect suggest about the elder's advice?

A. It is based on emotion rather than logic.

B. It is rushed and reactive.

C. It is cautious and carefully considered.

D. It focuses only on modern solutions.

Question 3: Which phrase best describes the meaning of polychronic signs as used in the passage?

A. written rules followed by the village council

B. warnings from religious leaders

C. one-time events used to justify rituals

D. multiple overlapping indicators that occur over time

Question 4: What does the elder's imperturbable demeanor reveal about his character?

A. He is easily swayed by the villagers' emotions.

B. He remains calm and composed despite conflict.

C. He is unaware of the villagers' frustration.

D. He enjoys stirring up disagreement.

Excellent! Tomorrow, we'll explore the subtle world of connotation and denotation.

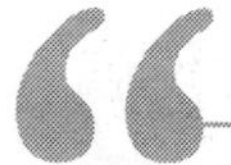

Understanding Connotation and Nuance

By the end of this lesson, you'll be able to:

- Distinguish between denotation and connotation in sophisticated vocabulary.
- Analyze how connotative meaning affects tone and the author's purpose.
- Identify semantic gradients among related terms.
- Select words with precise connotative shades for effective communication.

Key Concept #1: Denotation vs. Connotation

Why It Matters

Words carry two distinct levels of meaning: their literal definition (denotation) and their emotional associations (connotation). While a thesaurus might list words as synonyms based on denotation, their connotative differences can dramatically alter a text's impact. Understanding these subtle distinctions is essential for sophisticated reading and writing, allowing you to detect bias, interpret tone, and choose words with precision.

Mastering this skill helps you:

- Detect subtle bias in seemingly objective texts.
- Interpret literary tone and the author's attitude.
- Choose words with greater precision in your writing.
- Recognize manipulation in advertising and political language.
- Appreciate nuance in cross-cultural communication.

Analyzing Connotative Meaning

To identify connotative differences between words:

1. Identify the word's literal definition (denotation).
2. Consider the emotional associations it evokes (positive, negative, neutral).
3. Think about social or cultural attitudes linked to the word.
4. Compare it with synonyms to spot subtle differences in tone.
5. Notice how context might affect the word's connotative impact.

Example 1: Connotation in Character Description

Consider how different word choices with similar denotations create vastly different impressions of the same behavior:

Passage A: "Nev was **cautious** with his responses during the debate, **deliberating** carefully before addressing his opponent's points. His **economical** use of words reflected his **diplomatic** approach to controversial topics."

Passage B: "Nev was **hesitant** during the debate, **dawdling** before responding to his opponent's arguments. His **minimal** contribution of ideas demonstrated his **evasive** approach to controversial topics."

Both passages describe the same behavior—taking time before speaking and using few words—but create entirely different impressions:

- **cautious** (positive: prudent) vs. **hesitant** (negative: uncertain)
- **deliberating** (positive: thoughtful) vs. **dawdling** (negative: wasting time)
- **economical** (positive: efficient) vs. **minimal** (negative: insufficient)
- **diplomatic** (positive: tactful) vs. **evasive** (negative: avoiding)

The first passage portrays Nev as thoughtful and strategic; the second portrays him as indecisive and inadequate—all through connotative differences rather than factual distinctions.

Example 2: Connotation in Social and Political Language

Notice how terms with similar denotations carry dramatically different connotative implications:

Neutral Term	Positive Connotation	Negative Connotation
Confident	Self-assured	Arrogant
Careful	Prudent	Fearful
Persistent	Determined	Stubborn
Simple	Straightforward	Simplistic
Emotional	Passionate	Irrational
Traditional	Time-honored	Outdated
Unconventional	Innovative	Bizarre
Frugal	Thrifty	Cheap
Direct	Forthright	Blunt
Curious	Inquisitive	Nosy

These connotative differences often reveal subtle biases and attitudes. For instance, describing economic policies as "prudent" versus "fearful" significantly influences how readers perceive them, even when referring to identical measures.

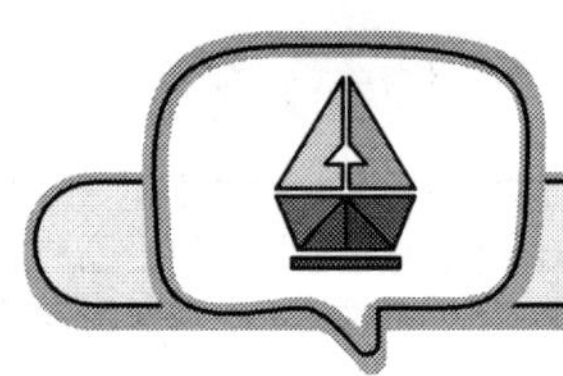

Week 1 • Practice Activity 1

Connotation Analysis

Directions: For each set of words below, all three have similar denotations but different connotations. Rank them from the most positive to the most negative connotation and explain the subtle differences in meaning.

1. stubborn / persistent / determined

Rank: ....

Explain the differences in meaning: ....

....

2. childish / childlike / youthful

Rank: ....

Explain the differences in meaning: ....

....

3. confident / conceited / self-assured

Rank: ....

Explain the differences in meaning: ....

....

4. thrifty / stingy / economical

Rank: ....

Explain the differences in meaning: ....

....

5. curious / inquisitive / nosy

Rank: ....

Explain the differences in meaning: ....

....

Key Concept #2: Understanding Nuance in Word Meanings

Why It Matters

Words rarely have single, fixed meanings—they contain subtle gradations and shades of significance that change with context. Understanding nuance in vocabulary allows you to perceive these finer distinctions and select words with greater precision. This awareness helps you recognize the carefully calibrated word choices authors make to convey exact meanings rather than approximate ones. In sophisticated texts, these nuanced distinctions often carry significant implications for interpretation.

Mastering this skill helps you:

- Distinguish between similar terms with subtle but important differences.
- Recognize how precise word choice shapes meaning in sophisticated texts.
- Select vocabulary with greater accuracy in your own writing.
- Appreciate the craftsmanship behind an author's specific word selections.

Analyzing Nuanced Language

Nuance refers to the subtle differences in meaning between similar words or phrases. These fine distinctions may involve intensity, specificity, attitude, or perspective, and they significantly affect how readers interpret a text.

When analyzing nuanced vocabulary, consider:

1. Specificity spectrum (general to precise)
2. Intensity gradations (mild to extreme)
3. Attitudinal shadings (approval to disapproval)
4. Field-specific connotations
5. Cultural and contextual implications

Understanding these subtle distinctions allows you to recognize when authors are using vocabulary with great precision to convey exact meanings rather than approximate ones.

Example 3: Gradations of Intensity and Meaning

When describing emotions or qualities, writers often select from a spectrum of related terms to convey precise degrees of intensity or specific aspects of an experience. Consider this analysis of terms describing sadness:

"After examining the patient's emotional state, Dr. Lin carefully selected her terminology in the assessment notes. The teenager was not merely 'sad' about his parents' divorce—a term too general to guide treatment. Nor was he experiencing 'depression,' which would suggest a clinical condition requiring possible medication. Instead, she documented that he appeared 'melancholic,' indicating a persistent, reflective sadness without the severe functional impairment of clinical depression. In their discussion, she noted his periods of 'despondency' following parental arguments, capturing the temporary feelings of hopelessness that accompanied specific triggering events."

This example demonstrates how terms within the same emotional family carry distinct implications:

- **Sad**: General feeling of unhappiness (low intensity, temporary)
- **Melancholic**: Reflective, persistent sadness (moderate intensity, ongoing)
- **Despondent**: Feeling hopeless (high intensity, typically triggered)
- **Depressed**: Clinical condition affecting functioning (high intensity, potentially requiring medical intervention)

Each term conveys not just different intensities but different qualities and implications of the emotional experience, allowing for much more precise communication than simply using "sad" repeatedly with modifiers.

Example 4: Cultural and Contextual Nuance

Words carry different implications depending on cultural context and the specific domains in which they're used. Consider how similar concepts take on distinct meanings across contexts:

"The architecture students debated restoration approaches for the historic building. Juan advocated for 'preservation,' arguing that the structure should be maintained in its current state with minimal intervention. Marcy instead supported 'conservation,' which would allow for careful repairs using traditional materials and techniques. Professor Hassan suggested 'rehabilitation' as a middle ground, permitting modern updates for functionality while respecting historical features. The city planner, however, pushed for 'renovation,' emphasizing the need for contemporary standards and economic viability.

Though the conversation seemed to circle around synonyms, each term represented a distinct philosophy with significant implications for the project's outcome. Their professor noted that these technical distinctions, while subtle to outsiders, formed the foundation of ethical practice in their field."

This example shows how terms that might appear interchangeable in everyday language carry precisely differentiated meanings in specialized contexts:

- **Preservation**: Maintaining the existing state with minimal changes
- **Conservation**: Protecting from harm while allowing careful restoration
- **Rehabilitation**: Updating for modern use while respecting historical character
- **Renovation**: Substantial modernization with less emphasis on historical authenticity

These nuanced distinctions reflect not just different processes but different values and priorities. Understanding these subtle differences allows both professionals and informed readers to recognize the significant implications behind seemingly similar terms.

Analyzing Nuanced Word Choices

Directions: Read the scientific excerpt below and answer the questions that follow.

Excerpt from "Rainforest Ecosystems: A South American Perspective"

The degradation of Amazonian rainforests represents an ecological crisis of unprecedented magnitude. What began as selective harvesting has escalated to widespread deforestation, transforming vibrant ecosystems into biological deserts. Indigenous communities, once the stewards of these lands, have been displaced by commercial interests seeking short-term financial gains at the expense of irreplaceable natural resources.

Scientific consensus confirms that these forests are not merely collections of trees but complex systems that regulate climate patterns. The moisture generated through evapotranspiration creates flying rivers that transport rainfall throughout the continent. As fragmentation of these forests continues, precipitation patterns become erratic, oscillating between devastating floods and prolonged droughts.

Conservation biologists propose various management strategies ranging from strict preservation to sustainable utilization. While preservationists advocate for untouched sanctuaries where natural processes proceed without human interference, pragmatists suggest that controlled human interaction may actually enhance biodiversity in certain contexts. Between these approaches lies a spectrum of possibilities that acknowledge both ecological imperatives and human necessities.

Question 1: What does the word degradation most likely suggest about the changes happening in Amazonian rainforests?

A. an increase in biodiversity over time

B. a shift toward natural forest regeneration

C. a harmful decline in the health and quality of the ecosystem

D. a seasonal pattern of vegetation loss

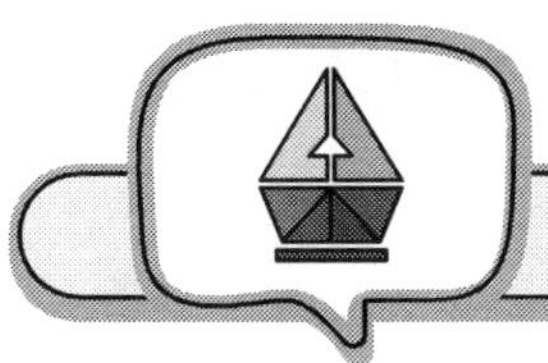

Question 2: What does the term evapotranspiration contribute to the meaning of the sentence: "The moisture generated through evapotranspiration creates flying rivers that transport rainfall throughout the continent"?

A. It describes how logging dries out forest soil.

B. It explains how water vapor from plants and soil enters the atmosphere.

C. It identifies a process that removes toxins from the rainforest.

D. It refers to artificial irrigation systems in tropical climates.

Question 3: Which phrase best explains the connotation of biological deserts in the passage?

A. places where sand has replaced plant life

B. forests that receive little sunlight due to thick canopies

C. landscapes temporarily cleared for farming

D. ecosystems that have lost nearly all biodiversity and ecological function

Question 4: What is the effect of using the phrase "a spectrum of possibilities" in the final paragraph?

A. It emphasizes the wide range of approaches between full preservation and human-managed use.

B. It shows that conservationists disagree on the value of rainforests.

C. It suggests there are only two effective conservation strategies.

D. It indicates that no current solutions fully address ecological needs.

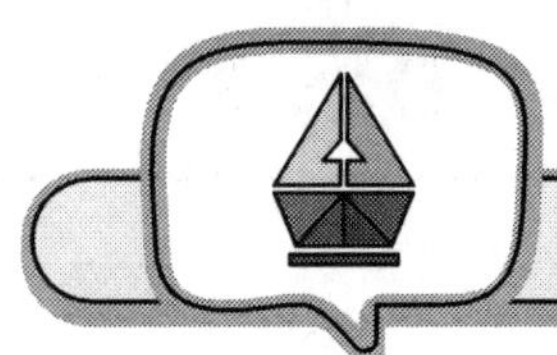

Analyzing Denotation, Connotation, and Nuance in Cultural Context

Directions: Read the excerpt below and answer the questions that follow.

Excerpt from "The Tale of Genji" by Murasaki Shikibu

The young prince's demeanor reflected a refinement that distinguished him among the courtiers. While others might be called handsome, his beauty transcended mere physical appearance, emanating from an inner harmony that even his detractors could not deny. His intellect was not that of a cold scholar, but rather displayed an elegant intelligence that manifested in his poetry and music.

When he spoke to the elder statesmen, he was neither servile nor presumptuous, finding that perfect balance that signified true nobility. The lesser courtiers witnessed his courtesy with wonder, for he extended the same thoughtful attention to them as he did to those of higher rank. Some whispered that such indiscriminate civility was calculated rather than genuine, yet even they could not resist his presence.

The emperor observed his son's graceful navigation of court politics with pride, though tinged with apprehension. Such perfection often invited jealousy, and indeed, certain ministers whose daughters had failed to capture the prince's interest had begun to scrutinize his actions with suspicious eyes. Yet it was difficult to find fault with one whose conduct was so impeccable, whose words were so carefully chosen, and whose aesthetic sensibilities so perfectly aligned with the imperial ideals.

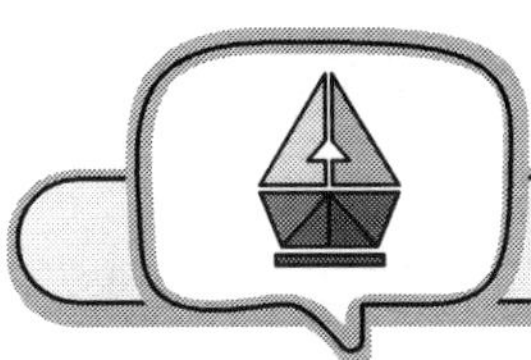

Week 1 • Practice Activity 3

Question 1: What is the connotation of the word refinement in the phrase, "The young prince's demeanor reflected a refinement that distinguished him among the courtiers"?

A. He behaved in an overly strict and disciplined way.

B. He lacked emotion and spontaneity.

C. He possessed an elegant, cultured grace beyond his peers.

D. He followed traditional rules without question.

Question 2: Which word in the passage best conveys a nuanced admiration for the prince's intellect, setting it apart from typical academic intelligence?

A. scholar

B. elegant

C. cold

D. mere

Question 3: What is the denotative meaning of the word servile as used in the sentence: "...he was neither servile nor presumptuous..."?

A. submissive or overly obedient

B. polite and well-mannered

C. arrogant and bold

D. dishonest or deceptive

Question 4: The phrase "indiscriminate civility" is used by some courtiers to describe the prince's behavior. What does this phrase most likely suggest about their cultural expectations?

A. Courtiers expected the prince to show more warmth to commoners.

B. Civility was not a valued trait in the court.

C. The prince should have been more assertive and confrontational.

D. They believed kindness should be reserved for those of high status.

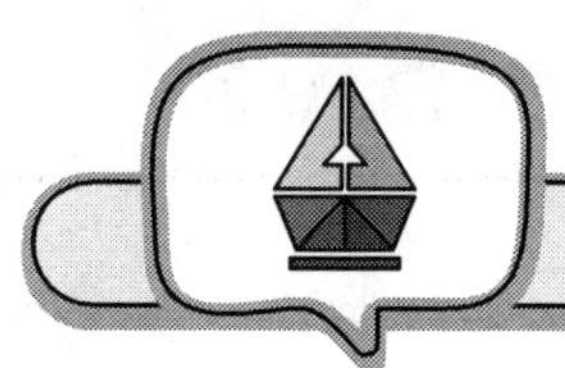

Week 1 • Final Reflection Questions

Directions: Take a few minutes to think about the lessons from this week, and then answer the questions below.

Question 1: Based on what you've learned this week about context clues, etymology, and connotation, which vocabulary development strategy do you find most valuable for your personal learning style?

Question 2: Consider a specific academic subject you're studying (science, history, literature, etc.). How might understanding word roots, prefixes, and suffixes help you master the specialized vocabulary in that subject area?

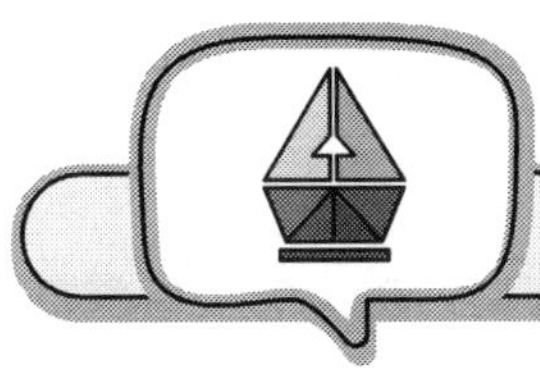

Week 1 • Final Reflection Questions

Fantastic job! You've now acquired powerful vocabulary strategies that will not only help you decipher challenging texts but also enable you to communicate with greater precision and depth in your own writing and thinking.

Final Thought:

The vocabulary skills you've developed this week are more than just academic exercises—they're intellectual tools that will serve you throughout high school and beyond. Rather than being intimidated by complex terminology in your readings, you now have strategic approaches to decode meaning through context, etymology, and connotation. This analytical approach transforms the way you process language, whether you're dissecting a literary classic, tackling a scientific journal, or preparing for standardized tests. More importantly, these skills enhance your ability to express your own ideas with precision and impact. As you move through more advanced coursework, the ability to distinguish subtle shades of meaning will increasingly set your thinking and writing apart. What you've learned isn't just about understanding difficult words—it's about engaging with language at a deeper level, where the true power of communication resides.

WEEK 2

Technical & Academic Vocabulary

Build skills to interpret specialized vocabulary across subjects. Understand how technical terms function in different fields and how precision shapes academic communication.

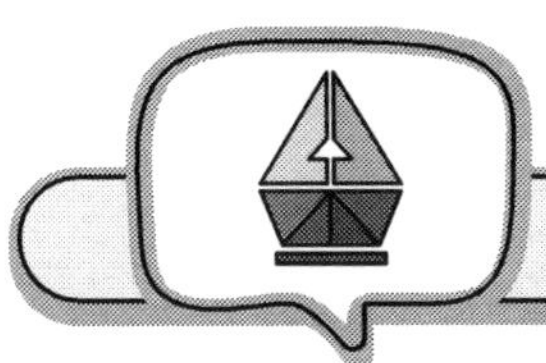

Introduction

This week, we'll explore the specialized language that experts use across different fields of study. You'll learn to identify and understand technical terms in scientific, historical, and academic texts from diverse cultural perspectives. By mastering domain-specific vocabulary, you'll gain access to more advanced material in subjects that interest you and develop the language skills needed for college-level work. These specialized terms aren't just "big words"—they're precise tools that experts use to communicate complex ideas efficiently. By the end of this week, you'll approach technical texts with greater confidence and precision.

Identifying Field-Specific Terminology

By the end of this lesson, you'll be able to:

- Recognize domain-specific vocabulary across different academic disciplines.
- Distinguish between general academic vocabulary and field-specific terms.
- Identify patterns in technical terminology across subject areas.
- Use contextual and structural clues to determine technical meanings.

Key Concept #1: Domain-Specific Vocabulary

Why It Matters

Every academic field and profession has its own specialized language—terms that have precise meanings within that discipline but may be unfamiliar to outsiders. This specialized vocabulary allows experts to communicate complex ideas efficiently, but it can create barriers for those unfamiliar with the terminology. Understanding how domain-specific vocabulary functions is essential for accessing advanced content in any field.

Mastering this skill helps you:

- Access higher-level texts in your areas of interest.
- Communicate more effectively in academic and professional settings.
- Develop a deeper understanding of complex concepts.
- Prepare for college-level coursework and future career paths.

Domain-Specific Language Across Fields

Domain-specific vocabulary refers to specialized words that are used in a particular subject or field. For example, in world history, terms like *feudalism*, *mercantilism*, and *cultural diffusion* have specific meanings that help explain historical systems and ideas. In chemistry, words like *covalent bond*, *molecule*, and *reactant* describe scientific processes and structures that wouldn't make sense the same way outside of science.

Example 1: Medical Terminology in Traditional Chinese Medicine

"The concept of qi represents the fundamental life energy flowing through meridians within the body. When qi becomes stagnant or imbalanced, various pathologies may develop. Practitioners use techniques such as acupuncture to stimulate specific acupoints along these meridians, restoring proper energy flow. Additionally, herbal formulations are prescribed to address patterns of disharmony, whether characterized by excess or deficiency. A thorough diagnosis requires examination of the pulse qualities and tongue appearance, which provide insight into internal conditions. The practitioner seeks to identify the underlying pattern rather than merely addressing symptomatic manifestations."

In this passage, terms like qi, meridians, acupoints, excess/deficiency (as specific diagnostic categories), and pulse qualities function as domain-specific vocabulary. While some words might be familiar in everyday usage, they carry precise technical meanings within Traditional Chinese Medicine that differ from their common definitions. These terms represent essential concepts that practitioners must understand to participate in the field's discourse.

Example 2: Economic Terminology in Historical Context

"The medieval *suq* functioned as more than a marketplace; it represented a complex economic ecosystem governed by principles of *mudaraba* and mutual benefit. Merchants operated under the *hisba* system, which regulated commercial activities according to community standards. Unlike European guild structures, the *futuwwa* associations integrated ethical conduct with commercial practice, emphasizing both expertise and moral character. The *waqf* institutions further supported economic development by providing infrastructure and services through charitable endowments. Together, these mechanisms created a distinctive approach to commercial exchange that balanced profit motives with social responsibility."

This passage contains specialized economic terminology (*suq*, *mudaraba*, *hisba*, *futuwwa*, *waqf*) from a Middle Eastern historical perspective. These terms represent economic concepts and institutions that were fundamental to commercial activity in this context but may be unfamiliar to those schooled only in Western economic traditions.

Key Concept #2: Identifying Technical Terms in Context

Why It Matters

Technical vocabulary often isn't explicitly defined in advanced texts, as authors assume readers have the necessary background knowledge. Developing strategies to identify and decipher these terms through context is essential for comprehending specialized material. By recognizing patterns in how technical terms are presented, you can more effectively navigate complex texts even when encountering unfamiliar terminology.

Mastering this skill helps you:

- Recognize when common words are being used in specialized ways.
- Identify key terms that require further investigation.
- Use contextual clues to determine technical meanings.
- Build specialized vocabulary more efficiently.

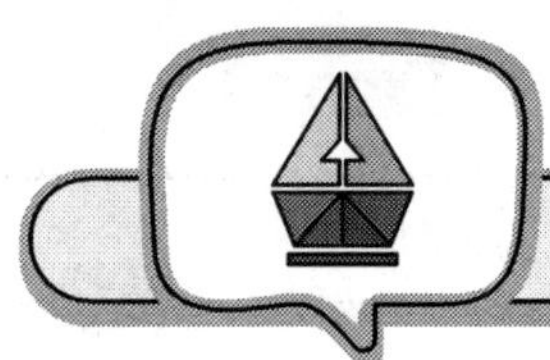

Strategies for Identifying Technical Terms

When reading academic or professional texts, technical terms often stand out because they carry meanings specific to a discipline. These words may include unfamiliar vocabulary, words with Latin or Greek roots, or everyday terms used in highly specific ways. To identify them, look for repeated terms that explain key processes, categories, or systems within the field, especially if they are central to the author's explanation or argument.

Example 3: Recognizing Technical Terms in Scientific Writing

"The *bioavailability* of herbal compounds depends on various factors, including molecular structure and administration route. Many traditional formulations contain *adjuvants* that enhance absorption or *synergistic components* that amplify therapeutic effects. Modern *pharmacokinetic* studies have confirmed that certain classical combinations increase the effective delivery of active constituents to target tissues. However, the complex interactions between multiple compounds present challenges for standardization and quality control protocols."

In scientific writing, technical terms often appear as:

- Nouns with specific prefixes/suffixes (*bio-availability*, *pharmaco-kinetic*)
- Terms that describe specialized processes or properties (*adjuvants*, *synergistic components*)
- Words that might have everyday meanings but carry precise scientific definitions

When reading scientific texts, watch for terms that appear repeatedly in discussions of specific phenomena, especially those that seem central to the main concepts being discussed.

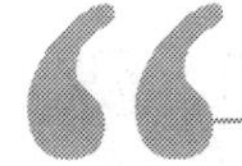

Example 4: Engineering Concepts in Historical Context

"Ancient Indian śilpa śāstras documented sophisticated architectural principles, including techniques for constructing self-supporting *corbelled arches* without requiring centering supports during construction. Engineers implemented precise *dimensional ratios* that ensured structural stability while embodying cosmological symbolism. The *trabeated system* employed beam-and-bracket methods that distributed load forces efficiently, allowing for expansive interior spaces. These structures demonstrated remarkable *seismic resilience*, with many withstanding earthquakes that destroyed newer buildings constructed using different methodologies."

In this engineering context, watch for:

- Terms naming specific structures or techniques (*corbelled arches*, *trabeated system*)
- Words describing specialized properties (*seismic resilience*)
- Measurements and standards (*dimensional ratios*)
- Foreign terms representing concepts without direct English equivalents (śilpa śāstras)

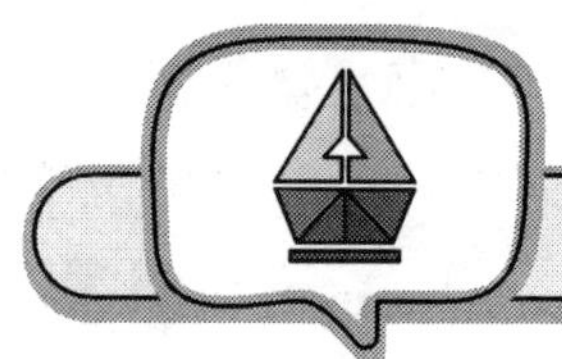

Identifying Domain-Specific Terminology

Directions: Read the following passages and then answer the questions that follow.

Passage A: Medical Research

Recent studies on neuroplasticity have revolutionized rehabilitation approaches for stroke patients. Functional MRI scans reveal increased cortical activation during constraint-induced movement therapy, where the unaffected limb is restricted to force engagement of the affected side. This method promotes neural reorganization through experience-dependent mechanisms, allowing alternative motor pathways to compensate for damaged circuits. The therapeutic window appears most favorable during the subacute phase, though significant improvements have been documented even in chronic cases when intervention intensity reaches sufficient thresholds.

Question 1: Which of the following best identifies neuroplasticity as a domain-specific term, and why is it essential to the overall meaning of the passage?

A. It refers to therapeutic exercises used after strokes and is commonly understood by the public.

B. It describes a general flexibility of the nervous system and can be used casually.

C. It is a neuroscience term referring to the brain's capacity to reorganize itself, which underlies the rationale for the therapy described.

D. It is a marketing term used to promote new therapy models for physical rehabilitation.

Question 2: What distinguishes constraint-induced movement therapy from general rehabilitation exercises based on the passage?

A. It targets psychological resilience through visualization and deep breathing.

B. It requires surgical intervention on the affected limb followed by therapy.

C. It focuses only on patients who are in the late stages of neurological decline.

D. It limits the use of the unaffected limb to intensify the use and recovery of the impaired side, encouraging cortical reorganization.

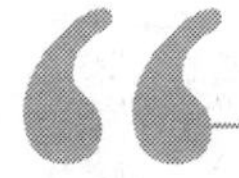

Question 3: Why is functional MRI considered a technical term, and what role does it play in the context of this passage?

A. It is a casual term used by patients to describe their progress in therapy.

B. It identifies a brain imaging technique used to track activity in specific regions, reinforcing the claim about cortical activation during therapy.

C. It refers to the measurement of heart rate and oxygen intake during physical therapy.

D. It is a broad label for any type of computerized medical equipment used in rehabilitation.

Question 4: In this medical context, the term subacute phase is best understood as:

A. a brief interval when a patient is healthy enough to begin basic training exercises

B. the period immediately before surgery, when symptoms are still mild

C. an intermediate recovery window post-stroke, where neurorehabilitation is most responsive due to ongoing but not yet stabilized neural adaptation

D. a long-term degenerative stage characterized by irreversible neurological damage

Question 5: What concept in the passage is most directly linked to the idea that experience can physically reshape brain function?

A. constraint-induced movement therapy

B. functional MRI

C. subacute phase

D. cortical activation

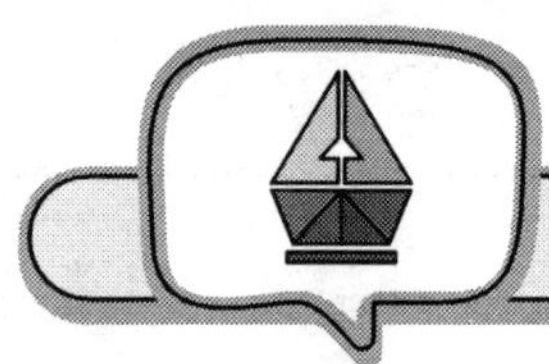

Passage B: Literary Analysis

The novel employs magical realism to explore post-colonial themes through a polyphonic narrative structure. The protagonist's internal monologues create cognitive dissonance with the omniscient narrator's account, highlighting the unreliability of historical documentation. Through this juxtaposition, the author subverts traditional bildungsroman conventions while incorporating elements of regional oral traditions. The resulting palimpsest of voices challenges hegemonic discourse about national identity while simultaneously constructing an alternative historiography that centers marginalized perspectives.

Question 6: Which of the following words from Passage B is domain-specific to literary analysis?

A. monologues

B. cognitive

C. polyphonic

D. perspectives

Question 7: In the passage, what does magical realism most likely refer to?

A. a genre that blends fantastical elements into realistic settings

B. a magical story told in a fantasy world

C. a novel that describes magic tricks and illusions

D. a theory of psychology applied to literature

Question 8: Which textual and contextual clues best support the interpretation of bildungsroman as a technical literary term?

A. It appears in quotation marks, indicating that it is a character's spoken word.

B. It is presented without translation, suggesting assumed knowledge of a recognized narrative form often studied in literary analysis.

C. It is listed among events in the plot, which implies it is part of the story's historical background.

D. It is compared directly to poetic devices, implying it is a stylistic technique rather than a genre.

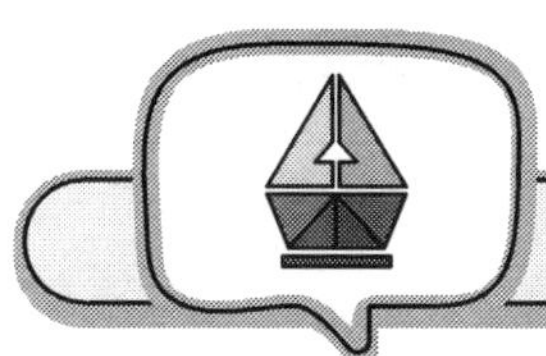

Question 9: In literary terms, what does the phrase palimpsest of voices most likely suggest about the form and thematic layering of the novel's narrative?

A. It describes the overlay of multiple narrative perspectives, evoking erased and rewritten histories that coexist and compete.

B. It reflects a formal convention in which one character dominates the storytelling, occasionally interrupted by footnotes.

C. It refers to a chronological retelling of events through a single voice, enhanced by sensory imagery.

D. It means the narrative relies on a circular structure with repeated motifs but no change in point of view.

Question 10: How does the phrase hegemonic discourse function within the analysis of the novel's treatment of national identity?

A. It critiques the overuse of formal language in contemporary fiction.

B. It points to the narrative's rejection of historical evidence in favor of personal emotion.

C. It emphasizes the positive cultural impact of government-supported educational campaigns.

D. It references a dominant ideology embedded in institutional narratives that suppress or marginalize alternative viewpoints.

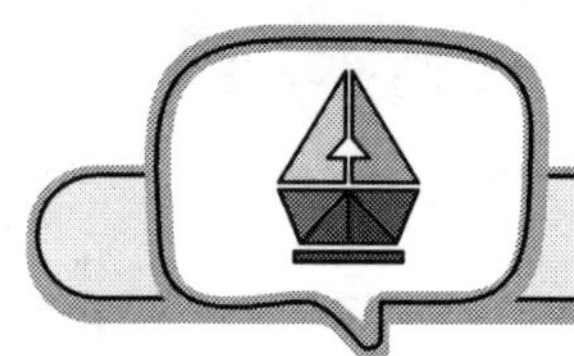

Analyzing Technical Text

Directions: Read the excerpt from this Chinese medical text and answer the questions that follow.

Excerpt from "Principles of Traditional Chinese Herbal Medicine"

Herbal formulations in traditional Chinese medicine follow specific principles of composition to achieve therapeutic efficacy. The primary herb, known as the *jun* (sovereign) component, addresses the main pattern of disharmony. Supporting herbs, called *chen* (minister) components, enhance the sovereign's action or address secondary aspects of the pattern. The *zuo* (assistant) herbs reduce toxicity, moderate harsh effects, or treat less prominent aspects of the condition. Finally, *shi* (envoy) herbs direct the formula's action to specific channels or harmonize the interactions between other components.

The classification of herbs according to their energetic properties—*hot*, *warm*, *neutral*, *cool*, and *cold*—determines their application for patterns of excess or deficiency. Heat-clearing herbs such as *Huang Lian* (Coptis) address conditions of pathogenic heat, while warming herbs like *Gan Jiang* (dried ginger) treat cold patterns. The herb's *flavor* (sweet, acrid, bitter, sour, or salty) further influences its functional direction and therapeutic action.

Diagnosis relies on the systematic analysis of *Eight Principles*: external/internal, hot/cold, excess/deficiency, and yin/yang. The practitioner examines pulse characteristics, tongue appearance, and other clinical manifestations to determine the underlying pattern rather than focusing solely on symptomatic presentation. This pattern differentiation (*bian zheng*) guides formula selection and modification according to individual patient requirements.

Question 1: What are the four categories of herbs in a traditional Chinese medicine formulation? How does each category function within the formula?

1. ....

....

2. ....

....

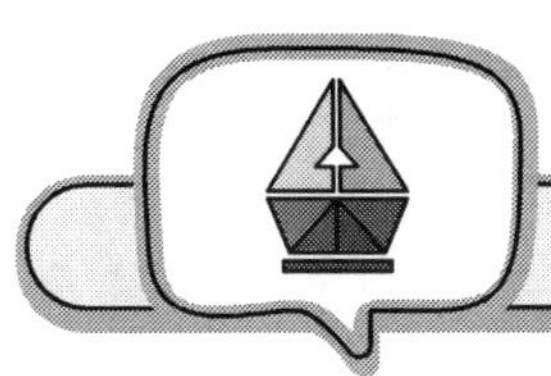

3. ....

....

4. ....

....

Question 2: Explain how the "Eight Principles" function as a diagnostic framework in traditional Chinese medicine. What makes this approach different from other medical systems?

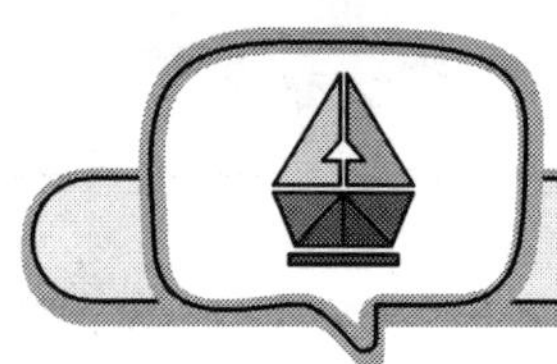

Cross-Cultural Technical Vocabulary

Directions: Read the excerpt about historical engineering concepts and answer the questions below.

Excerpt from "Engineering Principles in Classical Indian Architecture"

The architectural achievements of classical India represent sophisticated engineering solutions executed through a comprehensive technical knowledge system. The *vāstu śāstra* texts codified principles combining structural engineering with cosmological considerations, creating buildings that fulfilled both practical and symbolic functions.

The *mandala* grid system established proportional relationships that guided spatial organization and structural load distribution. Engineers implemented the *sandhāra prāsāda* design to create multi-tiered temples capable of supporting massive stone superstructures. The weight transfer mechanism relied on precisely calculated *garbhanyāsa* (foundation systems) that distributed forces through incrementally corbelled courses.

Stone elements were joined through various *bandha* (binding) techniques, including *vajra-bandha* (diamond-shaped interlocking joints) and *gaja-bandha* (mortise and tenon connections) that enhanced seismic resistance. The śikhara (superstructure) employed mathematical principles where each successive course projected slightly inward, creating self-supporting structures that distributed compressive forces optimally.

Water management systems incorporated *pranali* (drainage channels) and *somana* (water storage structures) that addressed seasonal monsoon conditions while providing year-round water access. These hydraulic systems demonstrated advanced understanding of fluid dynamics, particularly in step-well designs that maintained stable water temperature and accessibility regardless of fluctuating water tables.

Question 1: Which of the following terms from the passage refers to a foundational system used to distribute structural forces?

A. vajra-bandha

B. śikhara

C. garbhanyāsa

D. mandala

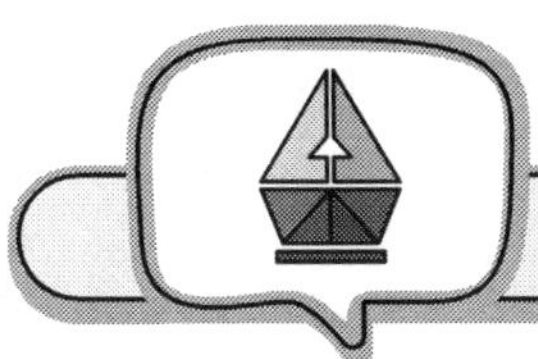

Week 2 • Practice Activity 3

Question 2: What does the term mandala grid system most likely refer to in the context of classical Indian architecture?

A. a spatial layout system that ensures proportional and structural balance

B. a decorative ceiling pattern

C. a symbolic diagram used only for religious rituals

D. a religious text explaining temple rituals

Question 3: Which statement best describes the function of bandha techniques such as vajra-bandha and gaja-bandha?

A. They are ornamental carvings used to decorate temple walls.

B. They are methods for attaching metal elements to stone surfaces.

C. They are architectural joining methods that enhance structural stability.

D. They are methods of painting used to mark ritual spaces.

Question 4: In the passage, the śikhara is described as a structure that:

A. channels water into storage systems

B. houses the inner sanctum of the temple

C. is built on the mandala grid's outer edges

D. uses mathematical design to remain stable and self-supporting

Question 5: Which of the following best explains the engineering challenge addressed by pranali and somana systems?

A. managing the temperature of the temple interiors

B. ensuring year-round access to water despite seasonal changes

C. deflecting sunlight from prayer halls

D. supporting acoustics for ritual chanting

Great job! Tomorrow, we'll explore academic vocabulary that crosses multiple disciplines.

Building Academic Vocabulary Knowledge

By the end of this lesson, you'll be able to:

- Recognize core academic vocabulary that appears across multiple disciplines.
- Distinguish between general and academic meanings of common words.
- Use academic vocabulary effectively in formal writing and discussion.
- Build your knowledge of Tier 2 vocabulary essential for academic success.

Key Concept #1: The Academic Word List

Why It Matters

Beyond field-specific terminology exists a core vocabulary of academic words that appear frequently across disciplines. Unlike everyday language or highly specialized terms, these "Tier 2" words create the framework for academic discourse across subjects. Research shows that understanding these words is critical for success in higher education and professional environments. These terms often have precise meanings in academic contexts that differ from their everyday usage.

Mastering this skill helps you:

- Understand complex instructions on assignments and exams.
- Access higher-level texts across all subject areas.
- Express ideas with greater precision in academic writing.
- Prepare for standardized tests that assess academic language.

Core Academic Vocabulary Across Disciplines

To identify core academic vocabulary, look for terms that:

1. Appear across multiple disciplines rather than in just one field.
2. Connect ideas and create a logical structure in academic writing.
3. Express intellectual processes, research methods, or analytical approaches.
4. Signal relationships between ideas (contrast, causality, sequence).
5. Express degrees of certainty, validity, or significance.

Example 1: Analyzing Academic Language in Historical Writing

"The political **paradigm** that **emerged** following the revolution **fundamentally** altered the relationship between citizens and the state. While some historians **attribute** this transformation to economic factors, others **emphasize** ideological influences. The **subsequent** development of constitutional governance **established** precedents that would **influence** regional politics for generations. **Despite** extensive documentation of official proceedings, the **perspectives** of ordinary citizens remain difficult to **ascertain** with certainty. This historical **analysis** attempts to **integrate** multiple sources to **construct** a more comprehensive understanding of this pivotal period."

The bolded words represent core academic vocabulary that appears frequently across disciplines. Unlike everyday conversational terms or specialized jargon, these words create the framework for academic discourse. Notice that many of these terms:

- Signal logical relationships (**despite**, **subsequently**)
- Describe intellectual processes (**analyze**, **integrate**, **construct**)
- Express degrees of certainty or emphasis (**fundamentally**, **ascertain**)
- Indicate causality or influence (**attribute**, **emerge**, **influence**)

These words often have more precise meanings in academic contexts than in everyday usage. For example, "construct" in academic writing typically means to build an argument or theory, not to physically build an object.

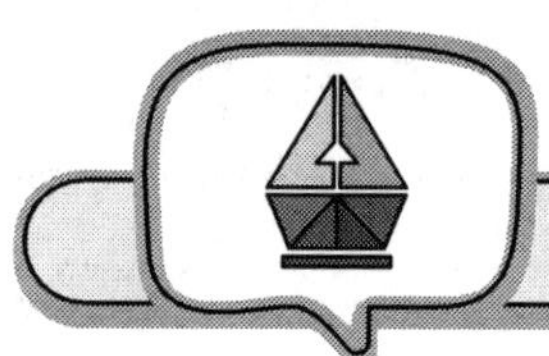

Example 2: Academic Vocabulary in Scientific Context

"Researchers **conducted** a longitudinal study to **investigate** the relationship between environmental factors and disease prevalence. The **initial** findings **indicated** a correlation, but further **analysis** was needed to **establish** causation. The team **devised** a new methodology to **address** potential confounding variables. This **approach yielded** more **robust** data, enabling the scientists to **formulate** a more **comprehensive** explanation of the observed patterns. Their **subsequent** publication **emphasized** the need for policy changes based on this **compelling** evidence."

Despite coming from a different discipline, this scientific text uses many of the same academic terms as the historical passage. Terms like **analysis**, **initial**, **approach**, and **subsequent** function as the connective tissue of academic discourse across fields. Recognizing and understanding these words allows you to access advanced content regardless of the specific subject area.

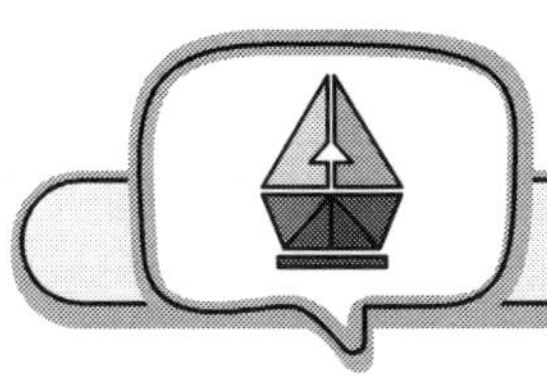

Week 2 • Practice Activity 1

Identifying Academic Vocabulary

Directions: Read the passage below and then answer the questions that follow.

Recent archaeological discoveries have challenged conventional interpretations of ancient migration patterns. Initial excavations indicated sporadic settlement, but subsequent analysis of ceramic fragments revealed consistent technological approaches across diverse geographic regions. Researchers have established a framework for evaluating cultural transmission based on these artifacts. This methodology integrates multiple data sources to construct a comprehensive understanding of population movements. Despite limited textual evidence, the archaeological data yields significant insights into social structures and economic systems. The emerging paradigm emphasizes regional interconnections rather than isolated cultural development. Further investigation will determine whether these patterns represent gradual diffusion or discrete migration events.

Question 1: In the sentence "Researchers have established a framework for evaluating cultural transmission...", what does the word framework most precisely suggest in the context of academic discourse?

A. a physical structure supporting artifacts

B. a loose outline used for storytelling

C. a set of building materials for reconstruction

D. a theoretical lens or system for interpreting data

Question 2: What is the effect of using the word "subsequent" in the phrase "subsequent analysis of ceramic fragments" rather than a simpler word like later?

A. It adds emphasis to the uncertainty of timing.

B. It reflects academic objectivity and chronological precision.

C. It indicates the analysis was unplanned.

D. It creates a casual tone appropriate for general audiences.

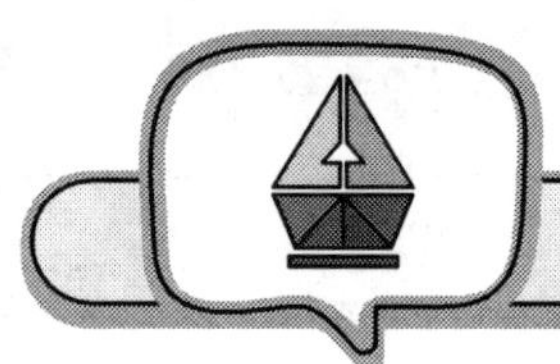

Week 2 • Practice Activity 1

Question 3: How does the term methodology function differently from method in the sentence "This methodology integrates multiple data sources..."?

- **A.** Methodology refers to the specific tools used in excavation.
- **B.** Methodology implies a broader theoretical and procedural framework than method.
- **C.** Methodology focuses only on laboratory techniques.
- **D.** There is no difference; both words are interchangeable in academic writing.

Question 4: In the context of "The emerging paradigm emphasizes regional interconnections...", which statement best captures the rhetorical purpose of the word paradigm?

- **A.** It introduces a proven hypothesis about cultural independence.
- **B.** It signals a temporary idea that will likely be revised.
- **C.** It implies a dominant, evolving model that reframes existing interpretations.
- **D.** It simply names a region being studied in the research.

Question 5: The word diffusion in the final sentence most likely contributes to the academic tone of the passage by:

- **A.** invoking a conceptual model of gradual, non-linear cultural exchange
- **B.** suggesting random and unpredictable migration patterns
- **C.** highlighting violent displacement and population collapse
- **D.** referencing a scientific term used loosely to describe cultural expansion

Key Concept #2: Shifts in Meaning Between Common and Academic Usage

Why It Matters

Many words have significantly different meanings in academic contexts than in everyday usage. These shifts in meaning can cause confusion when familiar words are used in specialized ways. Understanding how common words transform in academic settings helps you interpret texts more accurately and use vocabulary more precisely in your own academic writing.

Mastering this skill helps you:

- Avoid misinterpreting instructions and content.
- Use familiar words with appropriate precision in academic contexts.
- Recognize when common words carry specialized academic meanings.
- Improve the accuracy of your academic writing and discussions.

Common Words with Specialized Academic Meanings

To recognize meaning shifts in an academic context:

1. Be alert when familiar words appear in academic texts with seemingly subtle differences.
2. Notice when common words are used in patterns unusual for everyday speech.
3. Pay attention to words that seem to carry more precise or restricted meanings.
4. Look for familiar words being used in unexpected grammatical forms.
5. Consider whether the word has a specific technical meaning within the discipline.

Meaning Shifts in Academic Context

The chart below highlights how familiar words can take on more precise and technical meanings in academic contexts, which may differ significantly from their everyday usage.

Word	Everyday Meaning	Academic Meaning
theory	guess, hunch	well-substantiated explanation backed by evidence
significant	important, meaningful	statistically unlikely to occur by chance
argument	verbal disagreement	reasoned position supported by evidence
abstract	not concrete, conceptual	summary of a longer work
valid	acceptable, legitimate	logically sound based on proper reasoning
convention	gathering, meeting	established practice or rule in a field
principle	moral rule, belief	fundamental scientific law or concept
evaluate	judge, assess casually	systematically determine value or significance
model	miniature representation	theoretical framework explaining processes
bias	unfair prejudice	systematic error or tendency in research

Consider how the word "significant" functions differently in these two contexts:

- **Everyday usage:** "His graduation was a significant milestone in his life." Academic usage: "The results showed a significant difference between the experimental and control groups ($p<0.05$)."
- **In the academic context,** "significant" has a precise statistical meaning indicating that the observed difference is unlikely to be due to random chance. Understanding these distinctions is crucial for interpreting academic texts accurately.

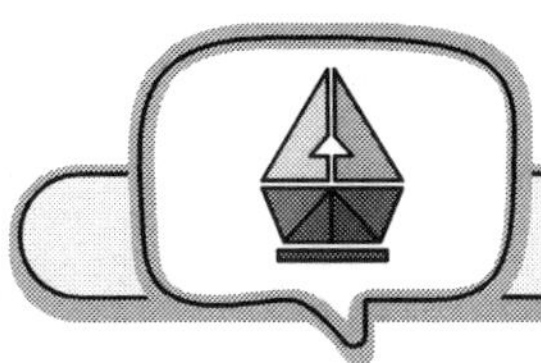

Example 3: Academic Meaning in Context

"The research team **evaluated** multiple theoretical **models** before selecting the most appropriate framework. Their methodology **addressed** potential sources of **bias** by implementing randomized selection procedures. The results revealed **significant** correlations between the variables, leading to a **valid** interpretation that **challenged** existing **conventions** in the field. The **abstract** of their paper clearly outlined the key **arguments** and supporting evidence, drawing attention to the **fundamental principles** that emerged from their investigation."

Each bolded word carries a specific academic meaning that differs from its everyday usage. For instance, "evaluated" here means a systematic assessment process rather than a casual judgment, while "models" refers to theoretical frameworks rather than physical replicas.

Note:

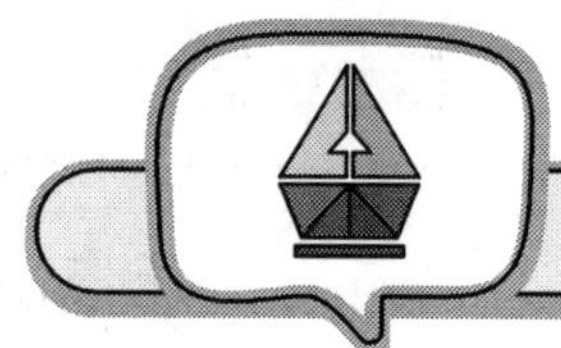

Week 2 • Practice Activity 2

Academic Word Meaning Shifts

Directions: Read the excerpt from this economic history text and answer the questions that follow.

Excerpt from "Economic Systems of the Medieval Middle East"

Economic historians have traditionally evaluated medieval commercial systems according to contemporary Western models of market development. This approach often distorts our understanding of alternative economic frameworks that operated according to different fundamental principles. A more valid methodology requires examining these systems within their specific cultural and religious contexts.

The concept of capital in the medieval Islamic economic sphere functioned within ethical parameters established by religious authorities. While investment and profit were legitimate pursuits, the prohibition against interest (riba) necessitated creative financial instruments that distributed risk and reward differently than European models. The mudaraba partnership, for instance, allocated financial capital and labor expertise between partners according to predetermined ratios, creating a significant distinction from fee-based lending systems.

Market regulation operated through the institution of hisba, which implemented practical oversight based on ethical principles. The muhtasib (market inspector) monitored transactions to prevent fraud, ensure standardized weights and measures, and maintain fair pricing. This regulatory framework integrated economic activity with broader social values rather than treating markets as autonomous entities governed solely by supply and demand dynamics.

Contemporary scholarship has constructed a more nuanced interpretation that acknowledges the sophistication of these alternative economic models. Rather than evaluating these systems as primitive precursors to modern capitalism, researchers now analyze them as coherent frameworks that addressed complex economic challenges through different institutional arrangements.

Question 1: Which of the following best explains how the term capital is used differently in the academic context of this passage than in everyday usage?

A. In everyday use, it refers to cities; here, it refers to financial assets used for investment.

B. In both uses, it refers to architecture and public buildings.

C. In everyday use, it refers to morality; here, it refers to religious scripture.

D. In both uses, it refers to something that holds symbolic power rather than material value.

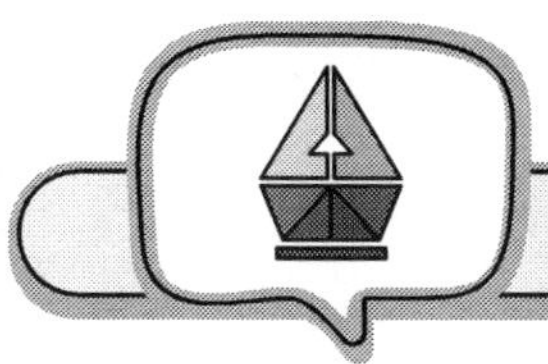

Week 2 • Practice Activity 2

Question 2: What is the effect of using the term mudaraba in the discussion of Islamic financial practices?

A. It introduces a general economic theory used throughout medieval Europe.

B. It highlights a religiously compliant investment model that contrasts with interest-based lending.

C. It suggests that partnerships in Islamic economies were informal and unregulated.

D. It implies that profit was forbidden in Islamic commercial systems.

Question 3: The term hisba in the context of the passage refers to:

A. a tax imposed on foreign merchants entering city markets

B. an economic philosophy of self-interest and free enterprise

C. a system of ethical market regulation based on religious principles

D. a type of legal code that only applied to rural communities

Question 4: In the final paragraph, how does the author use the phrase primitive precursors to modern capitalism?

A. to argue that Islamic economies were foundational to Western capitalism

B. to critique the bias of earlier historians who undervalued non-Western systems

C. to explain how European models improved upon medieval systems

D. to emphasize the similarities between Islamic and modern financial structures

Question 5: Which of the following terms best supports the passage's academic tone and central argument?

A. "contemporary" — used to describe modern-day economists

B. "autonomous" — used to praise free-market economies

C. "creative" — used to describe merchants' artistic expressions

D. "nuanced" — used to introduce a more layered understanding of past systems

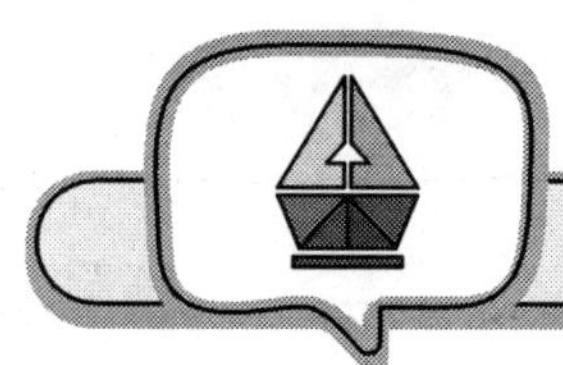

Week 2 • Practice Activity 3

Building Academic Vocabulary

Directions: Read the following paragraph and replace the underlined everyday language with more precise academic vocabulary.

My history paper looks at how people in ancient China came up with ways to deal with flooding. I think their methods were smart because they used the river's natural patterns instead of just trying to block the water completely. I found some good information showing that these techniques helped farming and also made trade easier between different areas. When you look closely at these water systems, you can see that they weren't just about stopping floods but also about making life better in many ways.

1. "looks at" - ....

2. "came up with" - ....

3. "smart" - ....

4. "used"- ....

5. "good"- ....

6. "helped"- ....

7. "made trade easier"- ....

8. "making life better"- ....

Wonderful work! Tomorrow, we'll practice applying technical vocabulary in context.

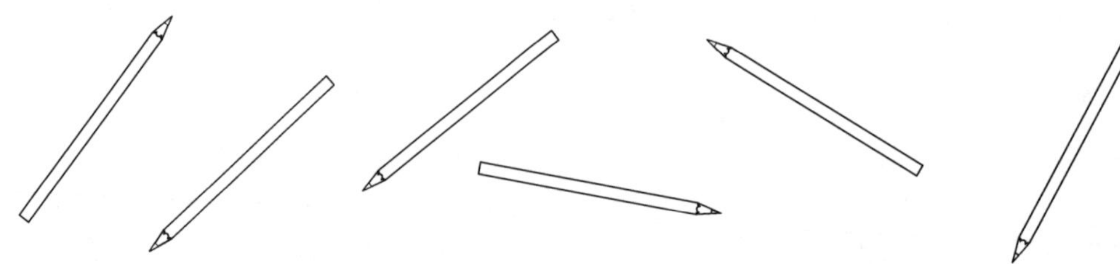

Understanding Technical Vocabulary in Context

By the end of this lesson, you'll be able to:

- Interpret specialized terminology accurately when reading technical texts.
- Recognize how context affects technical term meanings.
- Navigate complex texts containing multiple specialized vocabularies.
- Apply technical vocabulary knowledge to comprehend advanced reading material.

Key Concept #1: Interpreting Technical Precision in Context

Why It Matters

Technical terms often carry precise, specialized meanings that are crucial for accurate comprehension. In advanced texts, misinterpreting technical terminology can lead to fundamental misunderstandings of key concepts. Learning to interpret technical vocabulary accurately in context is essential for success in advanced courses and fields of study.

Mastering this skill helps you:

- Comprehend complex technical and academic passages.
- Distinguish between general and specialized uses of terms.
- Recognize nuanced meanings in specialized fields.
- Avoid misconceptions when reading advanced material.

Contextual Interpretation of Technical Terms

When approaching technical terms in reading, follow these steps:

1. Identify terms that appear to have specialized meanings.
2. Look for explicit definitions or explanations in the text.
3. Notice how the term relates to other technical vocabulary.
4. Consider how the discipline or field might affect the term's meaning.
5. Use context to refine your understanding of the term's specific usage.

Example 1: Interpreting Technical Terminology in Medical Texts

Consider this passage from a medical text and how context helps clarify technical terms:

"Patients presenting with acute myocardial infarction require immediate intervention to restore coronary perfusion. While thrombolytic therapy was once the standard treatment, primary percutaneous coronary intervention has demonstrated superior outcomes when performed within the recommended time window. The reduction in myocardial damage correlates directly with shorter door-to-balloon times, emphasizing the importance of streamlined emergency protocols."

In this medical context, understanding terms requires recognizing:

- Medical conditions (myocardial infarction = heart attack)
- Treatment approaches (thrombolytic therapy = clot-dissolving medication; percutaneous coronary intervention = catheter-based procedure)
- Measurement concepts (door-to-balloon time = time from hospital arrival to treatment)
- Physiological processes (coronary perfusion = blood flow to heart muscle)

The relationships between these terms in context help clarify their meanings. For example, the passage shows that "door-to-balloon time" must be a measure of treatment speed, since shorter times correlate with reduced damage.

Example 2: Interpreting Technical Terms in Cross-Cultural Context

"The traditional Chinese philosophy of medicine views disease as disruptions in the body's energetic balance. Diagnostic methods assess patterns of disharmony rather than isolated symptoms. For example, a practitioner examining a patient with digestive complaints would consider not only the gastrointestinal manifestations but also seemingly unrelated factors such as emotional state, sleep patterns, and tongue appearance. This approach reflects the holistic principle that organs and systems exist in constant dynamic relationships."

In this passage, contextual understanding requires recognizing:

- The conceptual framework ("energetic balance" as fundamental to health)
- How diagnostic terms function differently ("patterns of disharmony" rather than "isolated symptoms")
- The broader scope of relevant information (emotional state, sleep patterns as part of digestive diagnosis)
- The underlying philosophical principle (holistic interconnection of systems)

The context reveals that terms like "patterns," "balance," and "disharmony" carry specific technical meanings within this medical tradition that differ from their general usage or their use in Western medicine.

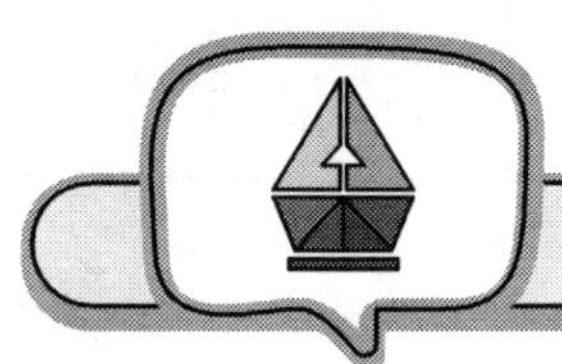

Technical Term Interpretation

Directions: Read the following excerpt from a chemistry textbook and then answer the questions that follow.

The bioactivity of curcumin, a polyphenolic compound derived from turmeric (Curcuma longa), has been attributed to its redox-modulating and anti-inflammatory properties. Curcumin's structure enables it to act as both a hydrogen donor and metal chelator, allowing it to scavenge reactive oxygen species (ROS) and inhibit lipid peroxidation. Its pharmacokinetic profile, however, is limited by poor aqueous solubility and rapid metabolic degradation via glucuronidation and sulfation in hepatic tissues. To address this, nanoparticle encapsulation and phospholipid complexation have been employed to enhance systemic bioavailability. Recent studies demonstrate curcumin's ability to modulate NF-κB signaling pathways and downregulate pro-inflammatory cytokines, suggesting therapeutic potential in oxidative stress–related pathologies. Ongoing research aims to elucidate the molecular interactions responsible for its pleiotropic effects across diverse biological systems.

Question 1: What does the term metal chelator most likely refer to in the context of curcumin's chemical activity?

A. a substance that breaks down metallic elements into gases

B. a compound that binds metal ions to prevent unwanted chemical reactions

C. a molecule that increases the absorption of metals in the body

D. a protein that transports metal atoms to muscle tissue

Question 2: In the sentence "Curcumin's structure enables it to scavenge reactive oxygen species (ROS)," what are reactive oxygen species?

A. stable molecules that improve cellular energy production

B. harmless byproducts of digestion

C. highly reactive molecules that can damage cells through oxidation

D. antibodies released during an allergic response

Question 3: What is the function of nanoparticle encapsulation as described in the passage?

- **A.** to protect curcumin molecules and improve their delivery and absorption in the body
- **B.** to increase the acidity of curcumin for faster metabolism
- **C.** to enhance curcumin's color for cosmetic use
- **D.** to convert curcumin into a solid metal compound for storage

Question 4: The passage mentions glucuronidation and sulfation as limiting factors in curcumin's pharmacokinetics. What does this imply about these processes?

- **A.** They prevent curcumin from breaking down in the liver.
- **B.** They improve the taste and texture of curcumin.
- **C.** They are metabolic pathways that rapidly degrade curcumin, reducing its effectiveness.
- **D.** They create new compounds that increase curcumin's potency.

Note:

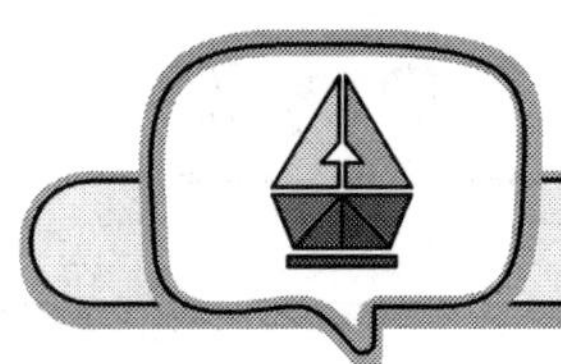

Week 2 • Practice Activity 2

Analyzing Technical Reading

Directions: Read the excerpt from a history text and answer the questions that follow.

In ancient Mesoamerica, the Maya civilization developed intricate calendrical systems that integrated astronomical observation with ritual governance. Using horizon-based alignments and zenithal sun tracking, Maya priests calibrated the Long Count calendar to predict cyclical phenomena such as solar eclipses, agricultural seasons, and dynastic anniversaries. These calculations were inscribed on stelae and codices, reflecting a worldview where cosmic order was inseparable from political legitimacy. The alignment of temple complexes with celestial events served not merely decorative purposes, but reinforced socio-religious authority and maintained ecological synchronicity with the annual monsoon patterns.

Question 1: What does the term zenithal sun tracking most likely refer to in the context of Maya astronomy?

- **A.** monitoring the phases of the moon to determine months
- **B.** using shadow lengths to predict winter and summer solstices
- **C.** measuring the sun's reflection on water to signal harvest times
- **D.** observing the sun when it passes directly overhead to mark seasonal shifts

Question 2: In the sentence "These calculations were inscribed on stelae and codices...", what does this detail suggest about Maya knowledge systems?

- **A.** They relied entirely on oral traditions with no written records.
- **B.** Their astronomical knowledge was preserved through durable and portable media.
- **C.** They used their writing systems mainly for trade and taxation.
- **D.** Their records were private and only kept in royal archives.

Question 3: How does the phrase cosmic order was inseparable from political legitimacy best explain Maya temple alignment practices?

A. Rulers demonstrated power by showing mastery of astronomy and aligning structures with celestial events.

B. Temples were randomly placed because geography mattered more than astronomy.

C. The calendar was primarily a military tool for organizing conquests.

D. Maya elites rejected astronomy in favor of imported religious models.

Question 4: What is the most accurate interpretation of the phrase ecological synchronicity with the annual monsoon patterns in this context?

A. Maya structures were only used during the rainy season.

B. Temple ceremonies caused rainfall through supernatural means.

C. The Maya calendar was timed to align human activity with natural environmental cycles.

D. Maya agriculture was based entirely on irrigation canals rather than seasonal weather.

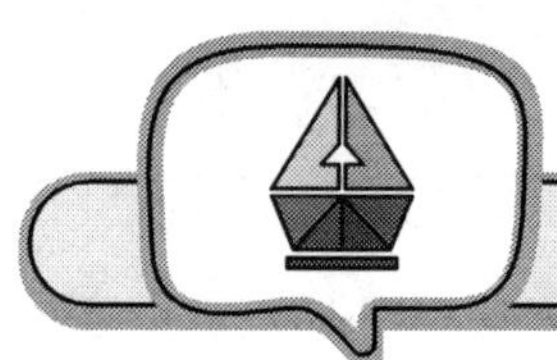

Key Concept #2: Navigating Multi-Disciplinary Vocabulary

Why It Matters

Many complex texts draw on terminology from multiple disciplines simultaneously. Environmental science combines biology, chemistry, and policy language. Medical humanities integrates medical terminology with philosophical concepts. Developing strategies to navigate these vocabulary intersections allows you to comprehend sophisticated texts that cross traditional disciplinary boundaries.

Mastering this skill helps you:

- Comprehend interdisciplinary texts that combine multiple technical vocabularies.
- Recognize when familiar terms are being used in unfamiliar ways.
- Track how concepts from different fields interact within a single text.
- Connect ideas across traditional subject boundaries.

Reading Strategies for Multi-Disciplinary Texts

When reading texts that combine vocabularies from different fields:

1. Identify which disciplines or fields are represented in the text.
2. Pay attention to terms that might have different meanings in different fields.
3. Use context to determine which disciplinary meaning applies.
4. Notice how concepts from different fields are connected within the text.
5. Look for "translation" moments where authors connect terms across disciplines.

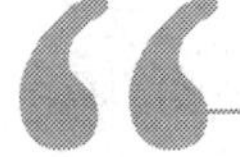

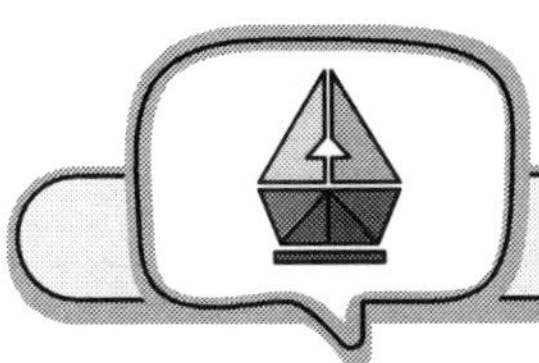

Example 3: Navigating Scientific and Policy Language

"The assessment of ecosystem services requires integrating ecological valuation with economic frameworks. While biodiversity metrics document the biological significance of habitats, policymakers require quantifiable cost-benefit analyses that translate ecological function into economic terms. The challenge lies in developing methodologies that neither reduce ecological complexity to simplistic monetary values nor remain too abstract for practical application in regulatory contexts. Recent approaches incorporating both direct use values and existence values have shown promise in bridging this conceptual divide."

This passage combines:

- Ecological terminology (ecosystem services, biodiversity metrics, ecological function)
- Economic concepts (valuation, cost-benefit analyses, direct use values)
- Policy language (regulatory contexts, methodologies, frameworks)

Understanding this text requires recognizing how terms function across these disciplines. For example, "value" has different meanings in ecological contexts (biological importance) versus economic ones (monetary worth). The passage discusses the challenge of translating concepts across these disciplinary boundaries.

Example 4: Reading Texts with Cultural and Technical Vocabulary

"Traditional water harvesting systems like the qanat technology of Persia represented sophisticated hydraulic engineering adapted to arid environments. These gravity-driven subterranean aqueducts tapped into aquifers at the base of highlands, then transported water through gently sloping tunnels to settlement areas. Unlike modern pumping systems, qanats operated within sustainable yield parameters, as extraction could not exceed the natural recharge rate of the aquifer. This inherent limitation embodied a cultural value system that prioritized intergenerational resource stewardship over short-term maximization."

This passage combines:

- Cultural/historical terminology (qanat technology, Persia)
- Engineering vocabulary (subterranean aqueducts, gravity-driven)
- Hydrological concepts (aquifers, sustainable yield, recharge rate)
- Environmental ethics terminology (intergenerational stewardship)

To fully comprehend this text, you must integrate understanding of the technical aspects of water engineering with the cultural context and values represented in the traditional approach.

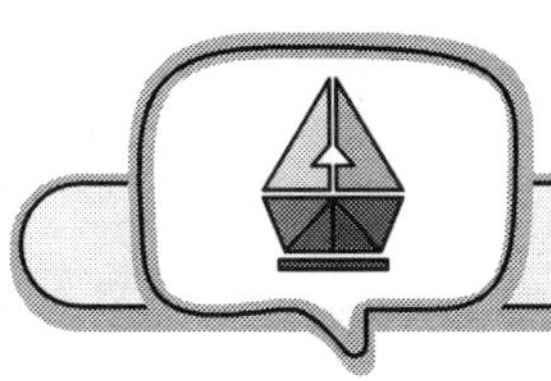

Week 2 • Practice Activity 3

Reading Interdisciplinary Technical Texts

Directions: Read the excerpt and answer the questions below.

Excerpt from "Bridging Science and Policy"

Efforts to mitigate anthropogenic climate change increasingly depend on the integration of scientific modeling, ecological forecasting, and legislative frameworks. Carbon sequestration, once considered solely a biochemical process, now functions as a cornerstone of climate policy, with governments implementing cap-and-trade programs to regulate industrial emissions. These market-based mechanisms assign economic value to atmospheric carbon, translating ecological stability into fiscal incentives.

However, policy implementation must also consider ecological thresholds and feedback loops. For instance, the degradation of keystone species in carbon-rich biomes such as peatlands or mangroves can trigger trophic cascades that undermine sequestration efforts. Meanwhile, chemists caution that abrupt shifts in ocean pH—driven by increased CO_2 solubility—may compromise marine carbon sinks by disrupting calcification processes in benthic organisms.

This convergence of biochemical, ecological, and regulatory discourse illustrates the need for transdisciplinary fluency. Environmental scientists must not only quantify emissions or model deforestation rates, but also navigate policy instruments and anticipate socio-economic trade-offs that influence global sustainability trajectories.

Question 1: In the passage, carbon sequestration is described as both a biochemical process and a policy tool. What does this dual function imply?

A. It is a marketing term used to promote sustainable agriculture.

B. It is a natural process that has no relevance to government action.

C. It only applies to ocean-based ecosystems.

D. It functions scientifically to store carbon and politically to regulate emissions.

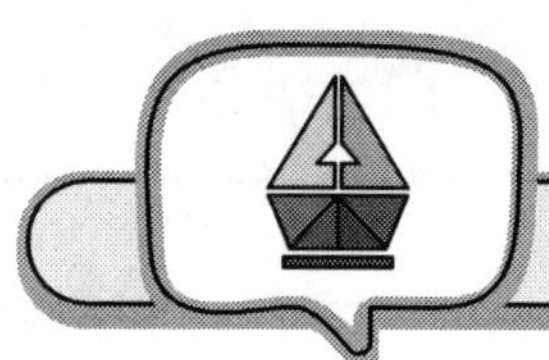

Week 2 • Practice Activity 3

Question 2: How does the term cap-and-trade function within the context of environmental policy?

- **A.** as a scientific method for calculating carbon absorption in forests
- **B.** as a legal mechanism for enforcing deforestation bans
- **C.** as a market-based system assigning economic value to carbon emissions
- **D.** as a chemical process for neutralizing airborne pollutants

Question 3: What does the phrase trophic cascades most likely refer to in the context of keystone species loss?

- **A.** a chain reaction in ecological systems triggered by changes in species populations
- **B.** a sudden change in climate patterns due to rising sea levels
- **C.** the buildup of pollutants in marine food chains
- **D.** a strategy for reintroducing endangered species to damaged ecosystems

Question 4: Why does the author mention ocean pH and calcification processes in benthic organisms?

- **A.** to show that marine life contributes to global warming
- **B.** to demonstrate that chemical changes in oceans can weaken natural carbon storage mechanisms
- **C.** to argue that chemistry is more important than ecology in climate policy
- **D.** to describe how artificial reefs are constructed for environmental protection

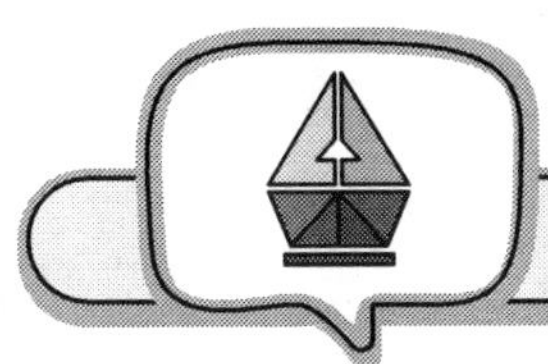

Week 2 • Final Reflection Questions

Directions: Take a few minutes to think about the lessons from this week, and then answer the questions below.

Question 1: Describe a time this week when you encountered a word that looked familiar but had a different meaning in an academic context. How did the context help you figure out its precise meaning? What strategies did you use to avoid misunderstanding the text?

Question 2: Explain how mastering academic vocabulary can help you not only read more advanced texts but also participate more effectively in higher-level discussions, writing, or research. How might this skill help you in your future academic or professional goals?

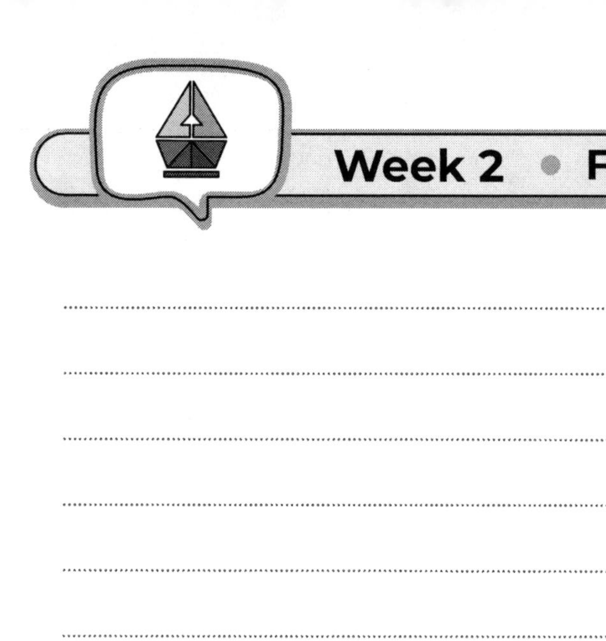

Week 2 • Final Reflection Questions

Excellent Effort! Next week, we will examine the relationships between words and how precise vocabulary choices shape meaning.

Final Thought:

The technical and academic vocabulary you've explored this week isn't just academic window dressing—it's the specialized language that allows experts to communicate precisely about complex subjects. Think of these terms as keys that unlock access to deeper knowledge in fields that interest you. When you understand domain-specific language, you move from being an outsider looking in to becoming an informed participant in sophisticated discussions. This transition is particularly powerful when exploring knowledge from diverse cultural perspectives, where technical vocabulary reveals alternative approaches to science, economics, and engineering that might not be covered in standard textbooks. As you continue building these vocabulary skills, you'll find yourself able to navigate increasingly specialized material with confidence, whether you're researching a topic that fascinates you, preparing for advanced coursework, or exploring career paths that require technical expertise.

WEEK 3

Word Relationships & Precision

Analyze relationships between words—like synonyms, antonyms, and analogies—and evaluate language precision. Explore how culture and history influence word meanings.

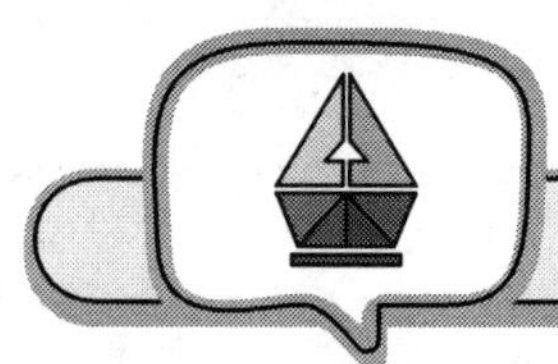

Introduction

This week, we'll explore the intricate relationships between words and how precise vocabulary choices shape meaning. By understanding how words connect through synonyms, antonyms, and more complex relationships, you'll develop a more sophisticated grasp of language. You'll also learn to evaluate word choices for precision and recognize how context influences meaning across different cultural perspectives. These skills will enhance both your reading comprehension and your ability to express ideas with greater nuance and clarity. By the end of this week, you'll approach texts with a deeper appreciation for the subtle connections and distinctions that give language its power.

Analyzing Word Relationships and Patterns

By the end of this lesson, you'll be able to:

- Identify and analyze different types of word relationships, including synonyms, antonyms, and analogies.
- Recognize semantic fields and how words group together conceptually.
- Use understanding of word relationships to enhance reading comprehension.
- Apply knowledge of word associations to determine the meanings of unfamiliar terms.

Key Concept #1: Types of Word Relationships

Why It Matters

Words don't exist in isolation—they form networks of meaning that help us understand language more deeply. Recognizing these relationships helps you decode unfamiliar vocabulary, understand nuanced meanings, and appreciate how authors create connections between ideas through their word choices.

Mastering this skill helps you:

- Determine the meanings of unfamiliar words by recognizing their relationships to known words.
- Develop more precise vocabulary for academic writing and discussion.

- Identify subtle connections between concepts in complex texts.
- Perform better on standardized tests that assess verbal reasoning.

Types of Semantic Relationships

Semantic simply means "relating to meaning in language." When we talk about semantic relationships, we're looking at how words connect to each other based on their meanings, not just how they sound or how they're spelled. Think of semantic relationships as the meaningful connections between words that create networks of understanding in your mind.

Word relationships form patterns that help us organize our understanding of language. Here are the primary types of relationships you'll encounter in sophisticated texts:

Example 1: Synonyms and Near-Synonyms

As you know, synonyms are words with similar meanings, but true synonyms (words with identical meanings) are actually rare. Most so-called synonyms are near-synonyms—words with similar but not identical meanings. Understanding these subtle distinctions is essential for precise communication.

Consider these near-synonyms describing intelligence:

"The professor was known for her **astute** observations about political systems, demonstrating an **incisive** mind that could cut through complex problems to identify core issues. Her colleagues admired her **sagacious** advice on departmental matters, while students appreciated her **perceptive** feedback on their essays. Even her critics acknowledged her **discerning** taste in selecting research topics."

These terms all relate to intelligence and insight, but each carries specific connotations:

- **Astute**: mentally sharp, especially regarding practical matters
- **Incisive**: penetrating and clear in thought or expression
- **Sagacious**: showing good judgment and wisdom, especially from experience
- **Perceptive**: having or showing sensitive insight
- **Discerning**: showing good judgment about quality or value

Understanding these distinctions allows readers to appreciate the precise qualities being described rather than simply registering a general sense of "smartness."

Example 2: Antonyms and Complementary Pairs

You already know that antonyms are words with opposite meanings, but there are several types of opposing relationships:

"The environmental conference featured both **optimistic** and **pessimistic** projections about climate change. Some speakers argued that technological solutions would be **sufficient**, while others insisted they were **inadequate**. The debate highlighted the **explicit** data from recent studies, though some implications remained **implicit**. Several proposed actions were deemed **mandatory** rather than **optional** if meaningful progress was to be achieved."

These pairs demonstrate different types of opposition:

- **Optimistic/pessimistic**: gradable antonyms (exist on a spectrum with middle values)
- **Sufficient/inadequate**: complementary pairs (mutually exclusive)
- **Explicit/implicit**: binary contrast (one quality or its absence)
- **Mandatory/optional**: relational opposites (opposed in relationship)

Recognizing these different types of opposition helps readers track the logical structure of arguments and understand the precise nature of contrasts being presented.

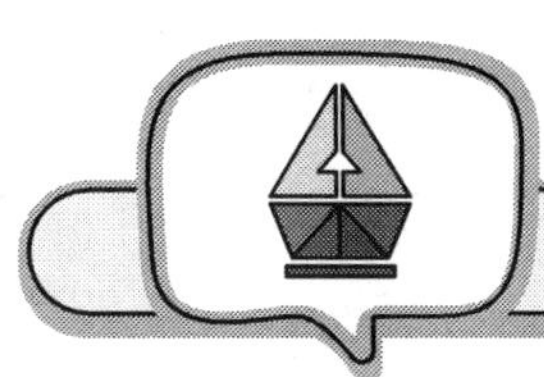

Week 3 • Practice Activity 1

Identifying Word Relationships

Directions: For each set of words below, identify the type of relationship (synonyms, antonyms, hyponym/hypernym, etc.) and explain the precise nature of the relationship.

1. benevolent, charitable, philanthropic, generous

Type of relationship: ....

Nature of the relationship: ....

....

....

2. revere, venerate, respect, honor

Type of relationship: ....

Nature of the relationship: ....

....

....

3. democracy, republic, monarchy, dictatorship

Type of relationship: ....

Nature of the relationship: ....

....

....

4. novel, poem, sonnet, haiku

Type of relationship: ....

Nature of the relationship: ....

....

....

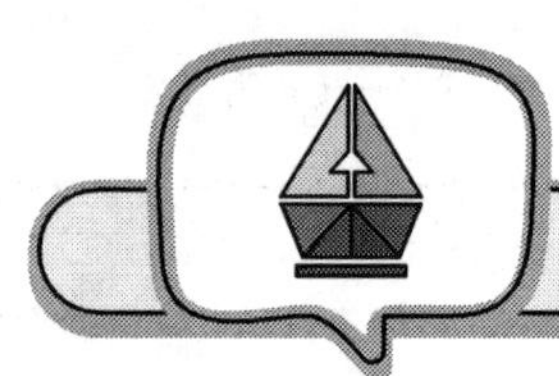

Week 3 • Practice Activity 1

5. ecstatic, elated, despondent, miserable

Type of relationship: ....

Nature of the relationship: ....

....

....

6. sprinting, jogging, walking, crawling

Type of relationship: ....

Nature of the relationship: ....

....

....

7. crimson, vermilion, scarlet, burgundy

Type of relationship: ....

Nature of the relationship: ....

....

....

8. computer, laptop, desktop, server

Type of relationship: ....

Nature of the relationship:

....

....

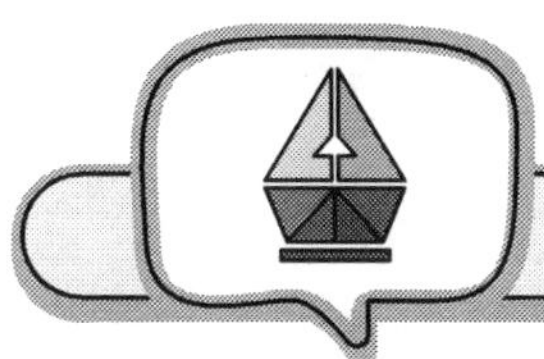

Key Concept #2: Complex Word Relationships

Why It Matters

Beyond simple similarities and differences, words form complex networks of meaning that organize our understanding of the world. Recognizing these sophisticated relationships helps you track conceptual connections in advanced texts and understand how different languages and cultures may organize meaning in distinct ways.

Mastering this skill helps you:

- Understand complex analogies in literature and academic writing.
- Recognize how words are organized hierarchically within semantic fields.
- Appreciate cultural differences in how languages categorize concepts.
- Make logical connections between ideas based on word relationships.

Complex Semantic Structures

Words form networks of meaning that help us make sense of the world around us. When we read, these relationships between words create patterns that can help us understand complex ideas. By recognizing how words connect to each other in different ways, you can better understand what you're reading and build a more sophisticated vocabulary. Let's look at several important ways words can relate to each other:

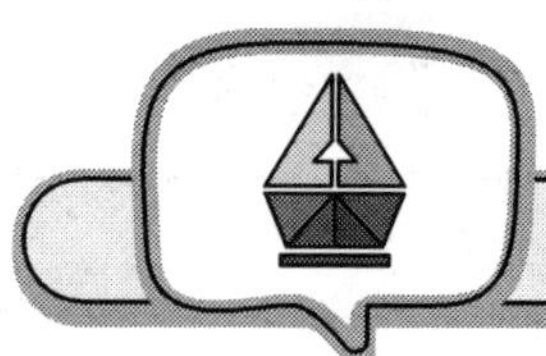

Example 3: Analogical Relationships

Analogies express relationships between pairs of words, often in the form "A is to B as C is to D." Understanding analogies requires identifying the precise relationship between the first pair of terms, then applying that same relationship to the second pair.

"The relationship between a **novelist** and a **character** parallels that between a **sculptor** and a **statue**. Both creators shape entities that exist in different realms of reality. Similarly, **democracy** relates to **citizens** as an **ecosystem** relates to **species**—both are systems whose health depends on the balanced interaction of constituent elements."

- A novelist is to a sculptor as one type of creator is to another, each shaping raw material—words or stone—into a meaningful form.
- A democracy is to an ecosystem as one type of system is to another, both functioning through dynamic interactions, balance, and constant adaptation.

Understanding analogies requires identifying the precise relationship in the first pair, then recognizing how that same relationship applies to the second pair, even in different domains of knowledge.

Example 4: Hyponyms and Hypernyms

Words exist in hierarchical relationships, with broader terms (hypernyms) encompassing more specific terms (hyponyms). These relationships create taxonomies that organize knowledge.

"The **coniferous forests** of Northern Europe differ markedly from the **deciduous woodlands** found further south, though both **ecosystems** support diverse **wildlife**. **Wolves** and **bears** once roamed these **forests** extensively, while smaller **predators** like **foxes** and **martens** remain common. Various **raptors**, including **eagles** and **hawks**, hunt in forest clearings, while **songbirds** such as **finches** and **warblers** inhabit the canopy."

This passage contains multiple hierarchical relationships:

- **Ecosystem** (hypernym) includes **forests** (hyponym), which include **coniferous forests** and **deciduous woodlands** (more specific hyponyms)
- **Wildlife** (hypernym) includes **predators** and **birds** (hyponyms)
- **Predators** (hypernym) include **wolves**, **bears**, **foxes**, and **martens** (hyponyms)
- **Birds** (hypernym) include **raptors** and **songbirds** (hyponyms)
- **Raptors** (hypernym) include **eagles** and **hawks** (hyponyms)
- **Songbirds** (hypernym) include **finches** and **warblers** (hyponyms)

Understanding these hierarchical relationships helps readers organize information and recognize how specific examples relate to broader categories.

Analyzing Word Relationships in Context

Directions: Read the paired passages and then answer the questions that follow.

Passage A: "Conservation Approaches in East Africa"

The concept of wildlife conservation in East African traditions differs fundamentally from Western preservation models. Rather than separating humans from nature, many indigenous communities practice sustainable coexistence. The Maasai, for example, have traditionally maintained the savanna ecosystem through controlled grazing practices that prevent bush encroachment. Their knowledge of seasonal migration patterns enables them to move their herds in harmony with wildlife movements.

This approach recognizes the interdependence between human livelihoods and ecosystem health. While modern conservation sometimes views pastoralists as threats to wildlife, traditional practices often serve as stewardship that maintains habitat diversity. The Maasai concept of enkiyio (sharing) extends beyond human communities to include relationships with wildlife and landscapes.

Contemporary conservation initiatives increasingly incorporate this indigenous knowledge, recognizing that exclusionary protection often fails without community support. The most successful programs combine scientific research with traditional ecological understanding, creating collaborative management approaches that honor both human needs and biodiversity preservation.

Passage B: "Forest Protection in Southeast Asia"

Forest conservation in Southeast Asian cultures has historically centered on spiritual and practical connections to forest ecosystems. In many traditional communities, forests are not viewed as wilderness to be preserved in an untouched state, but as sacred spaces requiring responsible stewardship. The concept of taboo forests in Indonesian traditions demonstrates how cultural practices can protect biodiversity through spiritual prohibitions against certain harvesting activities.

Indigenous forest management often includes a sophisticated understanding of ecological succession and species relationships. The Penan people of Borneo practice selective harvesting that maintains forest structure while meeting community needs. Their concept of molong—taking only what is needed while ensuring regeneration—represents a direct contrast to exploitative extraction that characterizes industrial forestry.

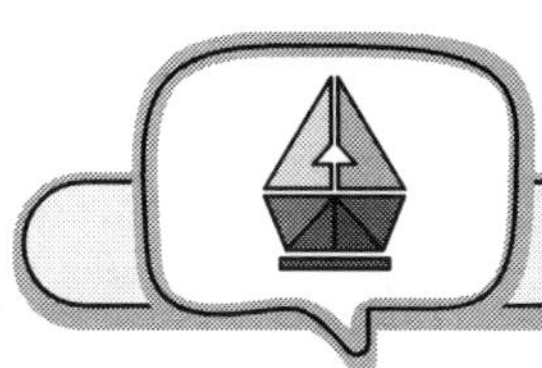

Week 3 • Practice Activity 2

Modern conservation efforts increasingly recognize the value of these traditional approaches. While early protection strategies often created conflict by excluding communities from ancestral lands, contemporary collaborative governance models incorporate indigenous perspectives. These partnerships acknowledge that sustainable utilization often proves more effective than strict preservation in maintaining forest biodiversity.

Question 1: Which of the following word pairs from the passages best represent near-synonyms that reflect similar ideas but emphasize different aspects of conservation?

A. Grazing and logging both describe the removal of natural resources.

B. Coexistence and stewardship both suggest human engagement with nature, though one focuses on mutual presence and the other on responsibility and care.

C. Wilderness and biodiversity both refer to untouched environments.

D. Taboo and science are both systems for organizing knowledge.

Question 2: Which word pair best illustrates a hierarchical relationship where one term refers to a broader category and the other to a specific example within that category?

A. Maasai and savanna: one is a community and the other a region.

B. Forest and molong: one is an ecosystem, and the other a conservation principle applied within it.

C. Controlled grazing and conservation: one is a specific practice within a broader environmental strategy.

D. Penan and Indonesia: one is a people and the other a country.

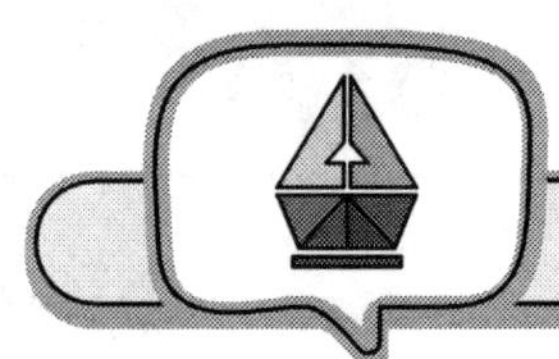

Question 3: Which of the following word pairs is most clearly used to contrast different conservation strategies discussed in the passages?

A. Sacred and spiritual: both reflect similar cultural values.

B. Indigenous knowledge and scientific research are presented as equally valid, but originate from different worldviews.

C. Exploitative extraction and selective harvesting: one implies unsustainable use, while the other reflects sustainable management.

D. Biodiversity and ecosystem both describe aspects of the natural world without opposing meanings.

Question 4: Which of the following best explains how the vocabulary in both passages reflects the cultural perspectives of indigenous communities toward nature?

A. Words like "regeneration" and "scientific modeling" emphasize data-driven environmental practices.

B. Terms such as "sharing," "taboo," and "sacred" convey relational and ethical views of nature rooted in cultural values and traditions.

C. Phrases like "preservation" and "exclusionary protection" suggest a focus on spiritual rituals rather than environmental policy.

D. The use of terms like "ecosystem" and "livelihood" shows that these communities treat nature purely as a resource for economic survival.

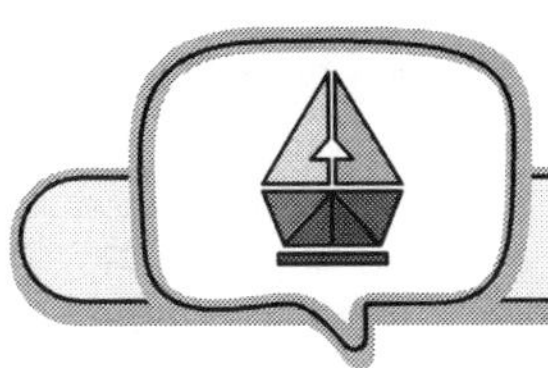

Word Relationships in Cultural Context

Directions: Read the excerpt from a classical Chinese poem and answer the questions about its word relationships.

"Autumn Reflections" (translated from classical Chinese)

The crimson leaves fall silently,
As azure skies embrace the mountain.
This melancholy season brings
Both joy and sorrow to my thoughts.
The wise hermit on the peak
Seems foolish to the merchant below.
Yet who can say which man truly
Understands life's transient beauty?
A gentle breeze now turns fierce,
Whispering secrets, then howling truths.
The ancient temple stands renewed
Each day by morning's golden light.
I ascend the winding path,
then Descend with newfound clarity.
The macrocosm of heaven reflected
In the microcosm of a dewdrop.

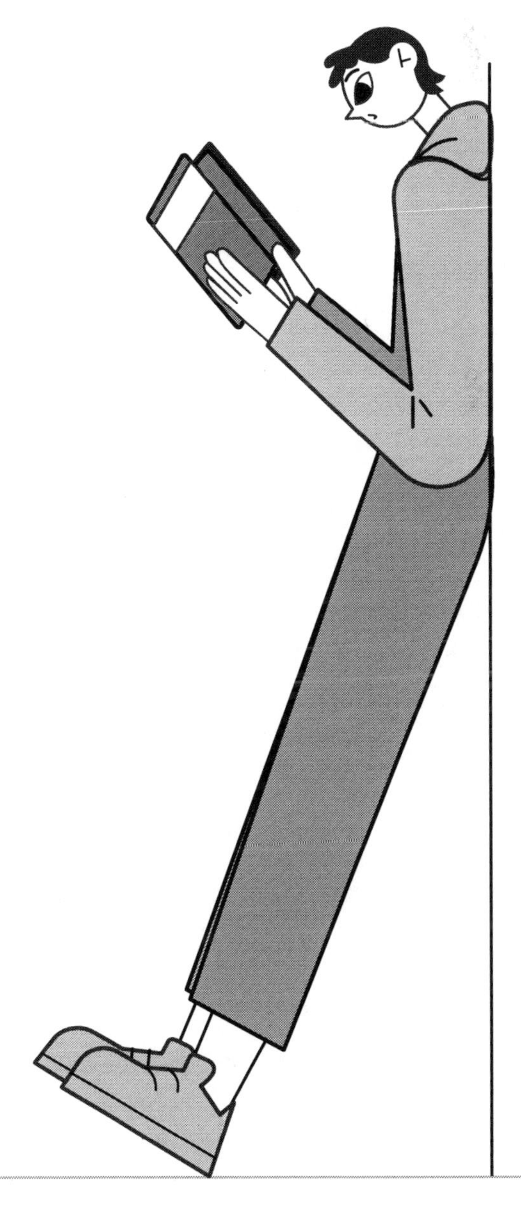

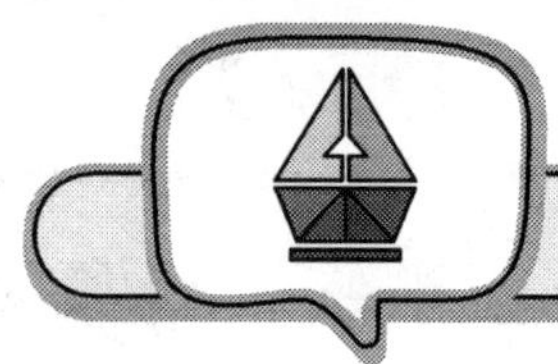

Week 3 • Practice Activity 3

Question 1: Which of the following word pairs from the poem best illustrate antonyms that reflect the poem's meditation on impermanence and duality?

A. "merchant" and "mountain" – contrasting economic and natural worlds

B. "joy" and "sorrow" – emotional opposites, highlighting the complexity of reflection

C. "dewdrop" and "golden light" – visual contrast used to describe beauty

D. "temple" and "hermit" – opposing social roles in religious settings

Question 2: How do the antonyms "ascend" and "descend" most contribute to the poem's philosophical message?

A. They create physical movement in the imagery but have no symbolic meaning.

B. They reflect the narrator's confusion and inability to reach clarity.

C. They suggest a journey that leads from outward exploration to inner enlightenment.

D. They refer to seasonal temperature shifts associated with autumn.

Question 3: Which of the following sets of words from the poem best belong to the semantic field of color, sound, and emotion, respectively?

A. "crimson," "howling," "clarity"

B. "azure," "whispering," "sorrow"

C. "golden," "fall," "joy"

D. "ancient," "fierce," "merchant"

Question 4: How do the poem's sensory details—especially related to color, sound, and emotion—enhance its meditation on nature and transience?

A. They provide concrete descriptions that distance the speaker from abstract ideas.

B. They root the reader in a single emotional tone of sadness and regret.

C. They blend natural imagery with shifting sensations to mirror the impermanence of life.

D. They focus the poem on one specific location rather than universal truths.

Awesome Work! Tomorrow, we'll explore how to evaluate precision in language use.

Evaluating Precision in Language

By the end of this lesson, you'll be able to:

- Distinguish between general and precise vocabulary in various contexts.
- Evaluate how specific word choices affect clarity and impact in a text.
- Recognize when authors deliberately use ambiguity or precision for effect.
- Analyze how language precision varies across different text types and purposes.

Key Concept #1: The Spectrum of Precision

Why It Matters

Precision in language involves selecting words that convey exactly the intended meaning. The difference between a general term and a precise one can dramatically affect a reader's understanding and the impact of a text. Learning to recognize and evaluate language precision helps you comprehend subtle distinctions in complex texts and express your own ideas with greater clarity.

Mastering this skill helps you:

- Recognize how specific word choices shape meaning in sophisticated texts.
- Evaluate the effectiveness of an author's language choices.
- Distinguish between deliberately vague and precisely detailed writing.
- Develop more nuanced and accurate expression in your own writing.

Evaluating Vocabulary Precision

In more difficult texts, authors carefully calibrate their language precision to serve their purpose. Understanding this spectrum from general to precise helps you evaluate word choices more effectively.

Example 1: General vs. Precise Vocabulary

General terms encompass broad categories, while precise terms target specific members of those categories with greater accuracy. Consider this spectrum of increasing precision:

General → Somewhat Specific → Highly Specific → Technical/Specialized

Let's examine how this works in descriptions of the same subject with different levels of precision:

- **Version 1 (General)**: "The **bird flew** from the **tree** and **ate** something from the **ground**."
- **Version 2 (More Precise)**: "The **hawk soared** from the **oak** and **seized** a **rodent** from the **meadow**."
- **Version 3 (Highly Precise)**: "The **red-tailed hawk launched** from the **white oak** and **captured** a **field mouse** in the **tallgrass prairie**."
- **Version 4 (Technical)**: "The juvenile **Buteo jamaicensis initiated hunting behavior** from its **Quercus alba** perch and **successfully predated** on **Microtus pennsylvanicus** in the **remnant prairie ecosystem**."

Each version provides increasingly specific information:

- Version 1 uses basic category terms (bird, tree) and general actions (flew, ate).
- Version 2 specifies type (hawk, oak) and more vivid actions (soared, seized).
- Version 3 provides exact species and habitat details.
- Version 4 uses scientific terminology for maximum precision.

The appropriate level of precision depends on purpose, audience, and context. A wildlife biology journal would require Version 3 or 4, while Version 1 might be suitable for a children's story. Recognizing these differences helps readers evaluate whether the author's precision level serves the text's purpose effectively.

Example 2: Precision and Purpose in Academic Writing

Academic writing generally requires high precision, but the specific type of precision varies by discipline and purpose. Compare these two academic passages:

History Text: "The **Treaty of Versailles** created conditions of economic **hardship** in Germany during the 1920s. The **reparation payments** mandated by the treaty, combined with the **hyperinflation** of 1923, contributed to widespread **political instability**. These factors provided fertile ground for the rise of **extremist ideologies** that promised simple solutions to complex problems."

Economics Text: "Post-war **monetary policy** in Germany led to an inflation rate exceeding **1,000,000%** by November 1923. The German mark devalued from 4.2 marks per dollar to 4.2 trillion marks per dollar. This **hyperinflationary spiral** effectively **eroded middle-class savings**, with particularly severe effects on **fixed-income pensioners** whose monthly stipends became worthless within days of receipt."

Both passages address similar historical events but employ different types of precision:

- The history text uses precise terminology for events and concepts, but remains somewhat general about economic conditions.
- The economics text includes specific numerical data, technical economic terms, and precise descriptions of financial impacts.

Each text's precision aligns with its disciplinary focus and purpose. The history text provides sufficient economic detail to understand broader political developments, while the economics text offers detailed financial analysis of the same period.

Analyzing Precision in Cultural Contexts

Directions: Read the excerpt on cultural traditions and answer the questions that follow.

Excerpt from "Navigating Time: Temporal Concepts Across Cultures"

Western industrialized societies conceptualize time as a linear progression, measured precisely by mechanical devices. Hours, minutes, and seconds regulate daily life, creating what anthropologists call monochronic time consciousness, where activities occur sequentially, and promptness holds moral weight. This temporal precision enables complex scheduling and coordination but often reduces time to a commodity that can be "spent," "saved," or "wasted."

In contrast, many Latin American cultures operate within what anthropologist Edward T. Hall termed polychronic time, where relationships take precedence over schedules. The Aymara people of the Andes have a spatial-temporal concept where the past is perceived as being "in front" (because it can be seen) while the future lies "behind" (because it cannot be seen)—a perspective embedded in their language, where the word nayra means both "past" and "eye/front."

The Maya developed multiple calendar systems of remarkable astronomical precision, including the tzolkin (260-day ritual calendar) and the haab (365-day solar calendar). However, their conception of time was cyclical rather than linear, with patterns of history expected to repeat in grand cycles. This perspective contrasts sharply with the Western notion of time as an arrow moving inexorably forward.

Many indigenous communities throughout Latin America observe natural temporality—time marked by ecological rhythms rather than arbitrary numerical divisions. Agricultural communities may measure time through seasonal indicators like flowering patterns or animal migrations. While less quantitatively precise than clock time, this approach often proves more relevant for activities dependent on environmental conditions.

The contemporary Latin American experience often involves navigating multiple temporal frameworks simultaneously. Urban professionals may operate on strict schedules in business contexts while maintaining more fluid time boundaries in family and community settings. This temporal flexibility represents not imprecision, but rather sophisticated adaptation to different social contexts and values.

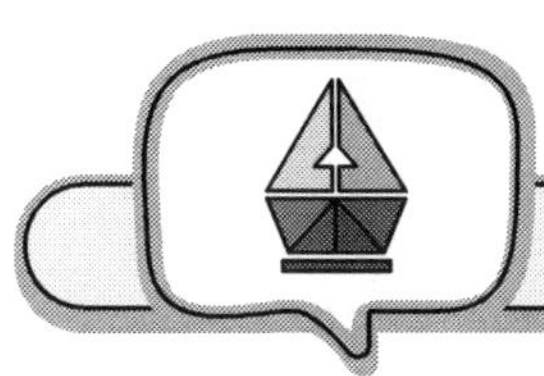

Week 3 • Practice Activity 1

Question 1: Identify three examples of precise terminology used to discuss time concepts in different cultures. How does this precision help the author make cross-cultural comparisons?

Question 2: The author uses both general terms and specific examples when discussing time. Explain how this balance of general and specific language helps communicate complex cultural concepts.

Key Concept #2: Ambiguity and Deliberate Imprecision

Why It Matters

While precision is often valued, authors sometimes deliberately use ambiguous or general language for specific purposes. Recognizing when imprecision is strategic rather than careless helps you understand an author's intentions and evaluate the effectiveness of their choices. This awareness also helps you appreciate literary techniques like symbolism and metaphor that depend on controlled ambiguity.

Mastering this skill helps you:

- Distinguish between ineffective vagueness and purposeful ambiguity.
- Appreciate literary techniques that depend on multiple possible interpretations.
- Recognize when general terms effectively communicate broader concepts.
- Develop critical awareness of how language can be manipulated for various purposes.

Strategic Imprecision and Ambiguity

Sometimes, less precise language serves legitimate purposes. Understanding when and why authors choose more general terms helps you evaluate language choices more accurately.

Example 3: Deliberate Ambiguity in Literary Texts

Literary writers often use ambiguity as a deliberate technique to create multiple layers of meaning or to engage readers in interpretation. Consider this poem excerpt:

"The **shadow** follows silently,

A **darkness** at my heels.

Its **whispers** haunt the corridors

Of all my waking hours."

The deliberately ambiguous terms (shadow, darkness, whispers) could represent many things: guilt, mortality, depression, fear, or past trauma. This ambiguity invites readers to engage with the text and find personal meaning. In this context, more precise terms would actually reduce the poem's effectiveness by limiting possible interpretations.

Example 4: General Terms for Broader Concepts

Sometimes, general terms effectively communicate broader concepts that specific terms would fragment:

"The concept of **justice** varies widely across cultural contexts. In some societies, **justice** emphasizes restoring communal harmony, while in others, **justice** focuses on punishment proportional to the offense. Many indigenous traditions view **justice** as inseparable from spiritual balance, whereas Western legal systems often separate **justice** from religious considerations."

Here, the general term "justice" serves as an umbrella concept that encompasses various cultural manifestations. Using more specific terms for each cultural understanding would obscure the paper's purpose of comparing different interpretations of the same broad concept.

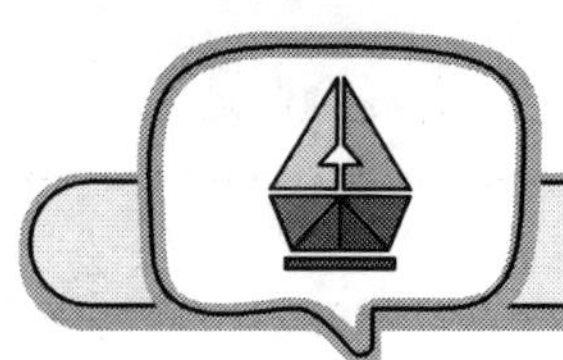

Week 3 • Practice Activity 2

Precision Analysis in Descriptive Writing

Directions: Read the descriptive passages below, each written with a different level of precision. Then answer the questions that follow.

Passage A (General Description) The mountain stood tall against the sky. Trees covered its slopes, and a river flowed nearby. Animals lived in the forest, and birds flew overhead. The weather changed throughout the year, making the landscape look different from season to season. People from the surrounding area visited the mountain for various reasons.

Passage B (Moderately Precise Description) The granite peak rose nearly ten thousand feet above sea level, dominating the western horizon. Pine and spruce forests blanketed the lower elevations, while a swift mountain stream carved a valley along the eastern face. Deer and elk inhabited the woodlands, and several raptor species nested in the cliffs. Summer brought wildflowers to the alpine meadows, while winter transformed the mountain with deep snowpack. Local residents and tourists frequented the trails for recreation and spiritual renewal.

Passage C (Highly Precise Description) Andesite and granite formations created the distinctive asymmetrical profile of Kanchenjunga, its jagged 8,586-meter summit perpetually snow-capped due to its elevation above the regional snow line. Old-growth Himalayan cedar and blue pine dominated the slopes between 2,500 and 3,800 meters, transitioning to rhododendron thickets and alpine scrub at higher elevations. The Tamur River, fed by glacial meltwater, descended through a V-shaped valley at a gradient of 15 meters per kilometer. The protected watershed harbored endangered red pandas and snow leopards, while lammergeiers and Himalayan griffons established nesting territories among the precipitous rock faces. During the pre-monsoon season (April-May), over 40 species of orchids bloomed in the middle elevations, creating a stark contrast to the January accumulation of approximately 3.5 meters of snow. For centuries, the Limbu people have conducted seasonal pilgrimages to sacred sites on the mountain's eastern aspect, while international mountaineering expeditions typically approach from the northwestern ridge.

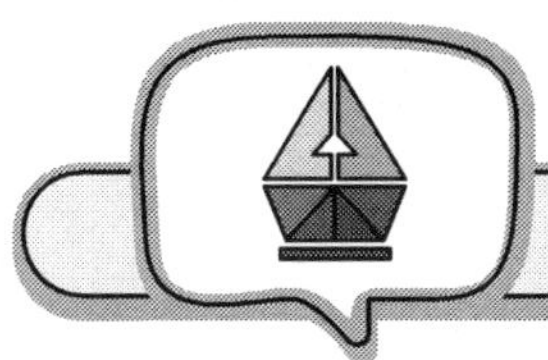

Week 3 • Practice Activity 2

Question 1: Which of the following words or phrases from Passage C best demonstrates a level of technical precision that surpasses the general language used in Passage A?

A. "The mountain stood tall."

B. "Pine and spruce forests blanketed the lower elevations."

C. "Jagged 8,586-meter summit perpetually snow-capped due to its elevation above the regional snow line."

D. "People from the surrounding area visited the mountain."

Question 2: Which of the following best explains why the phrase "over 40 species of orchids bloomed in the middle elevations" in Passage C is more precise than the seasonal references in Passages A and B?

A. It refers to plants rather than animals, making it more relevant to botany.

B. It gives an exact species count and timeframe, while the others use general seasonal terms like "summer" or "different from season to season."

C. It uses more poetic language than either Passage A or B.

D. It exaggerates the number of species to emphasize biodiversity.

Question 3: Which comparison below best illustrates the difference in level of detail and specificity between Passages B and C?

A. "Deer and elk inhabited the woodlands" (B) vs "Red pandas and snow leopards" (C) – C specifies rarer, endangered species with ecological importance.

B. "Trails for recreation" (B) vs "People visited the mountain" (A) – both show equal specificity.

C. "Snowpack" (B) vs "The weather changed throughout the year" (A) – both use precise scientific terminology.

D. "Granite peak" (B) vs "Granite formations" (C) – both indicate the same geologic insight.

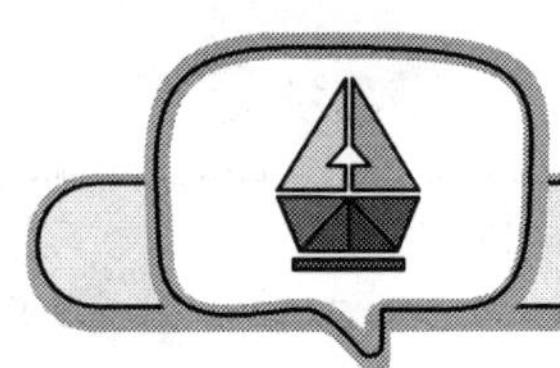

Week 3 • Practice Activity 1

Question 4: What feature of the phrase "Andesite and granite formations created the distinctive asymmetrical profile" most contributes to the high precision of Passage C?

A. It uses sensory imagery to describe the view from the summit.

B. It names specific types of rock and describes structural geometry not present in Passages A or B.

C. It focuses on the mountain's spiritual significance.

D. It refers to climate conditions affecting the terrain.

Fantastic! Tomorrow, we'll explore how context affects word meaning and usage.

Note:

Understanding Contextual Word Usage

By the end of this lesson, you'll be able to:

- Analyze how context determines and shifts word meanings.
- Recognize how cultural perspective influences vocabulary interpretation.
- Identify how the same words can carry different meanings across contexts.
- Apply contextual analysis to understand nuanced word usage in diverse texts.

Key Concept #1: How Context Shapes Meaning

Why It Matters

Words don't have fixed, unchanging meanings—their significance shifts based on surrounding words, cultural context, historical period, and the specific situation being described. Understanding how context determines meaning allows you to interpret texts more accurately and recognize when the same term carries different implications in different settings.

Mastering this skill helps you:

- Avoid misinterpretations based on a limited understanding of context.
- Appreciate how cultural and historical factors influence meaning.
- Recognize when familiar words are being used in unfamiliar ways.
- Develop greater sensitivity to nuance in sophisticated texts.

Contextual Meaning Across Texts

The way we understand words depends heavily on the context in which they appear. The same word can mean entirely different things depending on what surrounds it, who's using it, and where it appears.

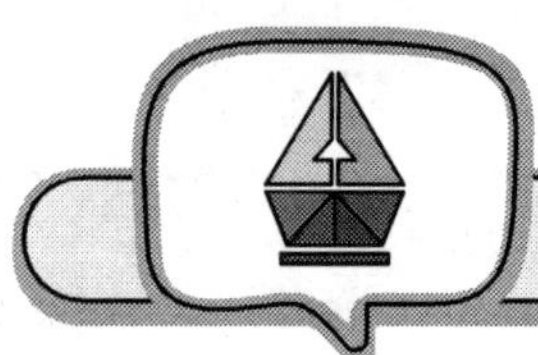

Example 1: Linguistic Context and Meaning

The words surrounding a term—its linguistic context—can dramatically alter its meaning. Consider how the word "commit" changes across these contexts:

- "The jury couldn't determine whether he had **committed** the crime."
- "She **committed** herself to improving her language skills."
- "The organization **committed** substantial resources to the project."
- "The psychiatric hospital can only **commit** patients who present a danger to themselves or others."
- "The journalist refused to **commit** to a specific political position."

In these sentences, "commit" variously means:

- To perpetrate or carry out (a crime)
- To pledge or dedicate oneself
- To allocate or assign (resources)
- To institutionalize someone involuntarily
- To align oneself with a viewpoint

Only by examining the surrounding words can we determine which meaning applies in each case. This linguistic context includes grammatical structures (commit + direct object vs. commit + reflexive pronoun), collocations (words commonly used together), and the broader subject matter being discussed.

Example 2: Cultural and Historical Context

Words also derive meaning from their cultural and historical settings. The same term may carry very different implications depending on cultural perspective or time period.

"Traditional Chinese medicine values **balance** as essential to health, viewing illness as resulting from disruptions in the body's natural equilibrium. The concept of **yin-yang balance** has influenced medical practice for thousands of years, with treatments designed to restore harmony between opposing forces. Western medicine historically emphasized identifying specific pathological **imbalances**—bacterial infections, hormonal irregularities, or genetic abnormalities—that could be targeted with precise interventions. Recent integrative approaches increasingly recognize the importance of **homeostasis** across body systems, acknowledging that **equilibrium** at the cellular, organ, and psychological levels contributes to overall wellness."

The concept of "balance" carries distinct meanings in different medical traditions:

- In traditional Chinese medicine: a holistic harmony between complementary forces
- In Western medicine (historically): the absence of specific measurable abnormalities
- In integrative medicine: the maintenance of optimal functioning across interconnected systems

Understanding these contextual differences prevents misinterpreting one tradition's concept of "balance" through the lens of another cultural framework.

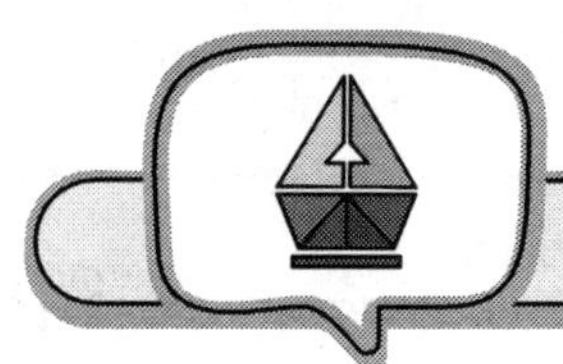

Week 3 • Practice Activity 1

Analyzing Contextual Meaning

Directions: Examine how the meaning of the bolded word changes across different contexts in each set. Explain the different meanings and what contextual factors create these differences.

Set A: "Culture"

1. The laboratory technician prepared a bacterial **culture** to identify the pathogen.
2. Japan's traditional tea ceremony reflects a **culture** that values mindfulness and precision.
3. The company worked to develop a **culture** of innovation among its employees.
4. They added yogurt **culture** to the milk to begin the fermentation process.

Explanation: ....

....

....

....

Set B: "Power"

1. The hurricane's destructive **power** left the coastal town in ruins.
2. The Constitution distributes **power** among the three branches of government.
3. The new solar panels generate enough **power** for the entire building.
4. Her moving speech had the **power** to change people's minds about the issue.
5. The teacher's understanding of classroom dynamics gave her the **power** to manage difficult students.

Explanation: ....

....

....

....

Key Concept #2: Cross-Cultural Vocabulary Interpretation

Why It Matters

When reading texts from diverse cultural perspectives, words that appear similar may represent quite different concepts. Culturally specific vocabulary often carries rich associations that don't translate perfectly between languages or worldviews. Developing sensitivity to these cultural dimensions of vocabulary helps you understand texts more deeply and avoid imposing familiar frameworks on unfamiliar concepts.

Mastering this skill helps you:

- Recognize culturally specific connotations in translated texts.
- Avoid oversimplified interpretations of complex cultural concepts.
- Appreciate linguistic diversity and its relationship to varied worldviews.
- Interpret global literature with greater cultural awareness.

Cultural Dimensions of Vocabulary

Words are embedded in cultural frameworks that shape their meanings in ways that may not be immediately apparent to outsiders. Understanding these cultural dimensions requires careful attention to context.

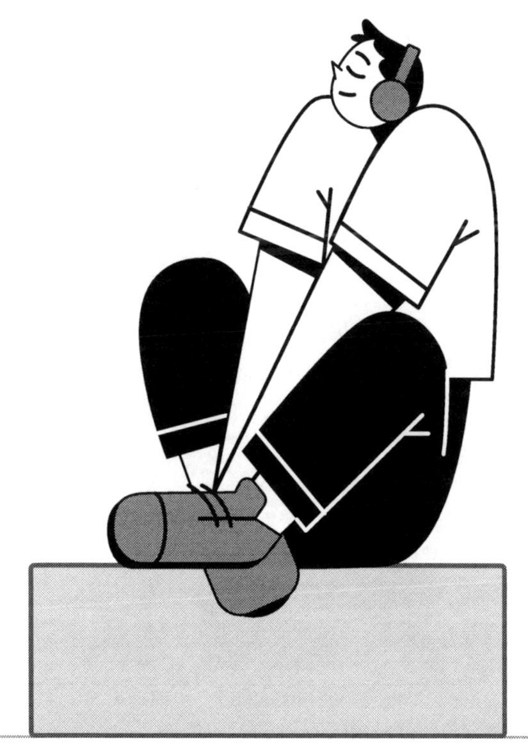

Example 3: Culturally Specific Concepts

Some terms represent concepts so culturally specific that they have no exact equivalents in other languages. These words can only be understood through careful explanation of their cultural context.

"The Andean concept of **ayni** fundamentally shaped community relationships and agricultural practices. Unlike simple reciprocity, **ayni** encompasses mutual obligation within a cosmic order where all elements—human, natural, and spiritual—participate in cycles of giving and receiving. When community members assist a family with planting or harvesting through **ayni**, they create not just practical support but a sacred bond reflecting the interconnectedness of all beings. This differs from Western notions of **cooperation** or **exchange**, which typically emphasize practical benefits or contractual relationships. Within the **ayni** framework, maintaining proper relationships becomes a spiritual as well as social responsibility, affecting everything from irrigation management to conflict resolution."

The passage demonstrates that while **ayni** might be approximately translated as "reciprocity" or "cooperation," these English terms fail to capture its spiritual dimensions and cosmic significance within Andean culture. Understanding **ayni** requires recognizing its distinctive features:

- Integration of practical, social, and spiritual dimensions
- Embeddedness in a specific cosmic worldview
- Extension beyond human relationships to encompass natural elements
- Moral and spiritual obligations beyond practical benefits

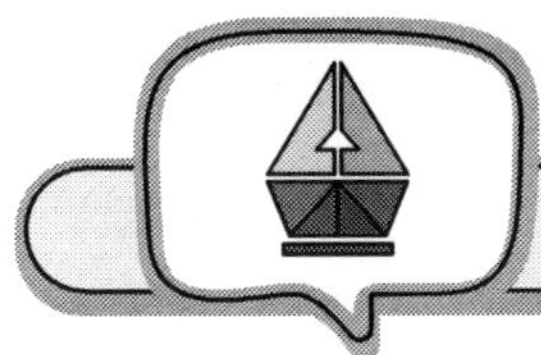

Example 4: Shifting Meanings Across Cultural Contexts

Even when the same word appears across cultures, its associations and implications may differ significantly based on cultural context.

"The concept of **family** varies dramatically across cultural contexts. In many Latin American cultures, **familia** typically extends beyond the nuclear unit to include grandparents, aunts, uncles, cousins, and even close non-relatives, who may share living spaces and participate in daily life. Important decisions often involve consultation with this extended **family** network. In contrast, the North American concept of **family** increasingly centers on the nuclear unit, with extended relatives playing more peripheral roles. East Asian understandings of **family** often emphasize hierarchical relationships and intergenerational obligations, with concepts like **filial piety** defining proper conduct toward parents and ancestors. The Arabic term **'aila** carries strong connotations of honor and collective identity that may not resonate as powerfully in more individualistic cultural contexts."

This passage highlights how the apparently universal concept of "family" carries different boundaries, expectations, and emotional associations across cultures:

- Latin American: extended, inclusive, collaborative decision-making
- North American: nuclear-centered, more individualistic
- East Asian: hierarchical, intergenerational, duty-oriented
- Arabic: honor-based, collective identity

Understanding these cultural variations prevents misinterpreting behaviors or values described in cross-cultural texts.

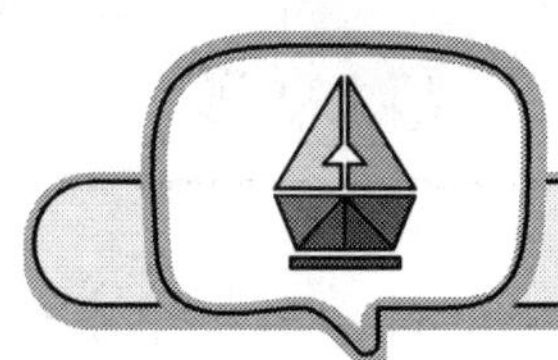

Week 3 • Practice Activity 2

Cultural Context Analysis

Directions: Read the paired passages on environmental conservation from African and Asian perspectives and answer the questions that follow.

Passage A: "Ubuntu and Environmental Ethics" (South African Perspective)

The philosophy of ubuntu—often expressed through the phrase "I am because we are"—extends beyond human relationships to encompass our connection with the natural world. Within this worldview, environmental conservation becomes not merely resource management but the maintenance of relationships that define our humanity. The concept of harmony in this context involves recognition that human well-being depends on the well-being of the larger community of beings.

Traditional conservation practices reflect this understanding. The Shona concept of muraramwa, for instance, designates sacred woodlands where harvesting is restricted through cultural protocols rather than legal enforcement. Similarly, totemic relationships with certain animal species created protection systems long before Western conservation models emerged.

Modern environmental challenges require approaches that honor this relational understanding while addressing contemporary pressures. The community-based natural resource management programs that have shown success in countries like Namibia and Zimbabwe draw strength from indigenous values while creating economic incentives aligned with conservation. These approaches recognize that sustainability must encompass cultural and spiritual dimensions, not just ecological and economic considerations.

Passage B: "The Way of Nature" (Japanese Perspective)

Japanese environmental thought centers on the concept of shizenkan—a view of nature not as something separate from humanity but as a relational field in which humans participate. Unlike Western conservation models that often begin with human-nature dualism, traditional Japanese approaches emphasize harmony (wa) within an integrated system where humans serve as stewards rather than rulers.

This philosophical foundation appears in practices like satoyama—the management of landscapes that blend cultivated fields, managed forests, and human settlements in a mosaic supporting both human needs and biodiversity. These traditional landscapes represent neither untouched wilderness nor completely domesticated space, but rather

a middle path maintaining balance between human use and ecological integrity.

Contemporary conservation efforts draw inspiration from these cultural values while addressing modern challenges. The Satoyama Initiative promotes landscapes where sustainable production practices support biological diversity. This approach recognizes that true sustainability requires maintaining the cultural practices and knowledge systems that have shaped human-nature relationships for centuries.

Question 1: In both passages, culturally specific terms like ubuntu and shizenkan are introduced. What is the primary function of these terms in the context of environmental ethics?

A. They describe ancient legal codes used to regulate natural resources.

B. They illustrate how religious beliefs override environmental decisions.

C. They ground conservation philosophies in relational worldviews that emphasize interconnectedness between humans and nature.

D. They are examples of modern Western ecological theories adapted by other cultures.

Question 2: Both passages reference the concept of harmony in South African and Japanese contexts. How do the meanings of harmony differ in these two philosophical traditions?

A. In the South African view, harmony refers to legal protection of sacred spaces, while in the Japanese view, it refers to detachment from nature.

B. In the South African context, harmony emphasizes spiritual kinship with nature, while in the Japanese context, it emphasizes functional integration within managed landscapes.

C. In both contexts, harmony means avoiding any human impact on ecosystems.

D. In both contexts, harmony is viewed as a scientific process measured through biodiversity indices.

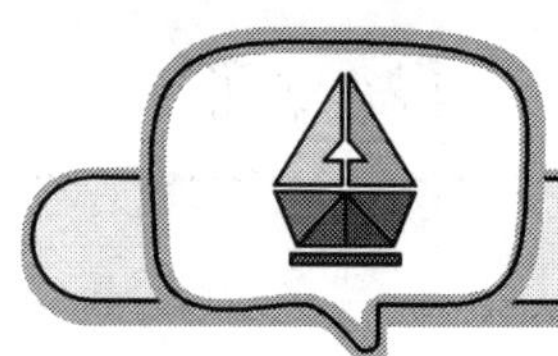

Week 3 • Practice Activity 2

Question 3: How do the paired terms muraramwa and satoyama reflect differing approaches to environmental space?

A. Muraramwa refers to untouched wilderness, while satoyama represents industrial farmland.

B. Muraramwa is a legal category, while satoyama is a philosophical metaphor.

C. Muraramwa embodies culturally protected sacred land, while Satoyama reflects integrated, semi-managed ecosystems that blend human activity with ecological health.

D. Muraramwa is a term rooted in Western land management, while satoyama refers to post-war urban design.

Question 4: What do both passages suggest about the role of indigenous or traditional knowledge in contemporary conservation efforts?

A. It is outdated and often contradicts modern science.

B. It provides cultural legitimacy but lacks ecological effectiveness.

C. It serves as a complementary framework that informs community-based and sustainable conservation models.

D. It is relevant only in isolated rural areas, not in broader policy discussions.

Question 5: In Passage B, what does the phrase "a middle path maintaining balance between human use and ecological integrity" most likely mean?

A. a literal path created for hikers and tourists in protected areas

B. a philosophical approach that avoids extremes, aiming for coexistence rather than domination or exclusion

C. a transitional zone where forest boundaries are fenced off from farmland

D. a government-imposed compromise between developers and environmental activists

Context in Literary Expression

Directions: Read the excerpt from this Latin American essay and answer the questions about contextual word usage.

Excerpt from "Memory and Identity in Latin American Narratives"

Our concept of tiempo transcends the mechanical march of minutes and hours. For us, time flows differently—circling back upon itself, connecting us to our ancestors through shared rituals and stories that make the past perpetually present. When the abuela tells stories of revolution on starlit evenings, the events of decades ago become immediate, woven into the fabric of today's reality.

The Western notion of progress—that linear advance toward some imagined future perfection—often feels foreign to our cyclical understanding. Our communities measure development not by technological acquisition or economic indicators, but by the strength of human connections and the preservation of ancestral knowledge. True wealth resides in relationships, in belonging, in the ability to share what one has rather than accumulate what one does not need.

Even our understanding of space differs from the colonial grid that attempted to impose order on our landscapes. Our territories are defined not by property lines but by memory, by the stories attached to mountains and rivers, by the sacred places where the boundaries between worlds grow thin. A home extends beyond physical walls to encompass community lands and the paths connecting extended families across distances.

The contemporary struggle for identity occurs at this cultural crossroads, where global forces push toward homogenization while local traditions insist on the value of difference. Our language itself becomes a battleground—Spanish words carrying indigenous structures, indigenous terms expressing concepts no European tongue can fully capture. This linguistic mestizaje reflects our larger cultural reality, where seemingly contradictory elements coexist, creating something entirely new yet anchored in ancient foundations.

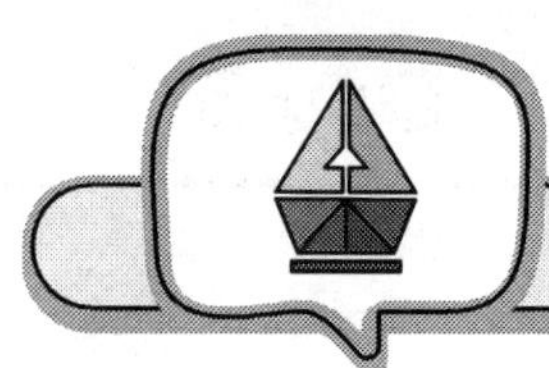

Week 3 • Practice Activity 3

Question 1: The author uses the Spanish word "tiempo" alongside the English word "time." How does context suggest these terms might carry different meanings or associations?

Question 2: Identify a word whose meanings in this cultural context differ from their common Western interpretations. Explain the contextual factors that create these differences.

Question 3: How does the author use contrasting contexts to highlight different cultural understandings? Give specific examples from the text.

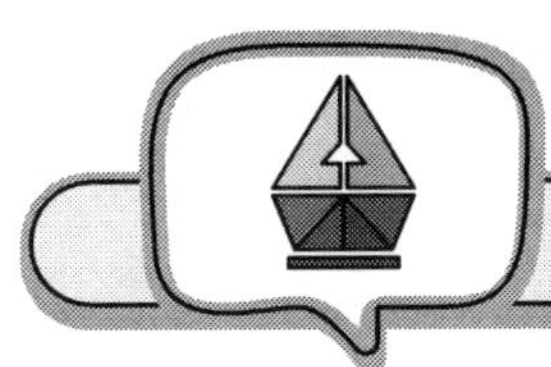

Day 3

Week 3 • Final Reflection Questions

Directions: Take a few minutes to think about the lessons from this week, and then answer the questions below.

Question 1: If you were to teach someone how to recognize nuanced word meanings in a poem or historical text, what's one technique from this week that you would share—and why?

Question 2: After exploring precision in language, do you think ambiguity can ever be more effective than clarity?

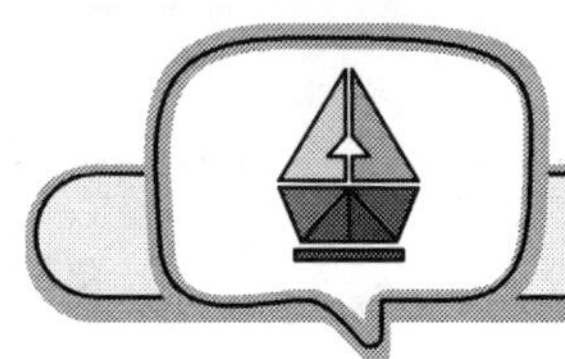

Week 3 • Final Reflection Questions

Great job! Next week, we will take what we have learned about vocabulary and apply it to SAT and ACT strategies.

Final Thought

This week has transformed how you understand words by revealing the complex relationships between them. You now know that words don't exist in isolation but form networks of meaning through synonyms, antonyms, and hierarchical relationships. You've learned to appreciate the power of precise language while recognizing when ambiguity serves a purpose. Most importantly, you've discovered how context—linguistic, cultural, and historical—shapes meaning in ways dictionaries can't capture. These skills make you a more perceptive reader and precise communicator, able to navigate subtle distinctions in meaning across diverse texts. As you encounter challenging readings in literature, science, or social studies, you'll now approach them with a deeper awareness of how words create meaning together, not just individually. This understanding of language as a complex, context-dependent system will serve you well in all your academic pursuits and beyond.

WEEK 4

SAT/ACT Vocabulary Strategies

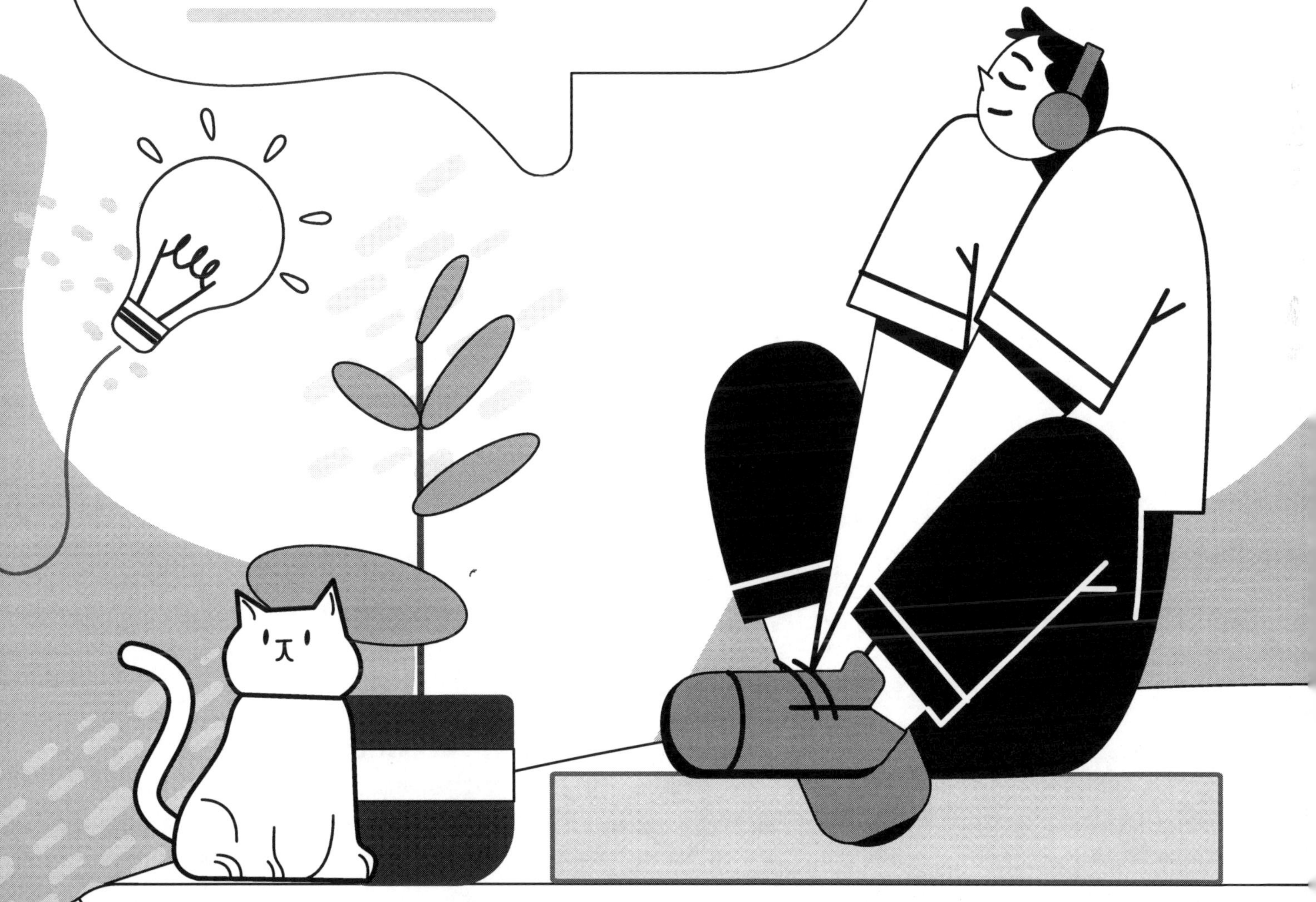

Master vocabulary-in-context strategies for standardized tests. Practice breaking down unfamiliar words using context, roots, and smart elimination while avoiding test traps.

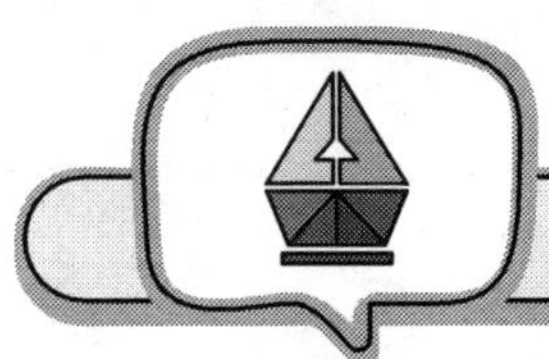

Week 4 • SAT/ACT Vocabulary Strategies

Introduction

This week, we'll focus on strategies specifically designed to help you tackle vocabulary challenges on standardized tests like the SAT and ACT. While these tests no longer include direct vocabulary questions like "antonym" or "synonym" sections, they still assess your vocabulary knowledge through reading comprehension passages and questions about words in context. You'll learn practical approaches for determining word meanings, dealing with unfamiliar terms, and applying vocabulary skills under test conditions. By mastering these strategies, you'll not only improve your test scores but also develop reading skills that will benefit you across all subjects. By the end of this week, you'll approach vocabulary questions with greater confidence and precision.

Mastering Vocabulary in Context Questions

By the end of this lesson, you'll be able to:

- Identify common types of vocabulary-in-context questions on standardized tests.
- Apply specific strategies to determine the correct meaning of words in test passages.
- Recognize when a familiar word is being used in an unfamiliar way.
- Avoid common traps and misconceptions in vocabulary questions.

Key Concept #1: Understanding Vocabulary-in-Context Questions

Why It Matters

On the SAT and ACT, vocabulary questions typically ask about the meaning of a word as it's used in a specific passage. The challenge is that these questions often focus on common words with multiple meanings, where the correct answer depends entirely on how the word functions in that particular context. Learning to analyze these questions systematically helps you avoid making assumptions based on the word's more familiar definitions.

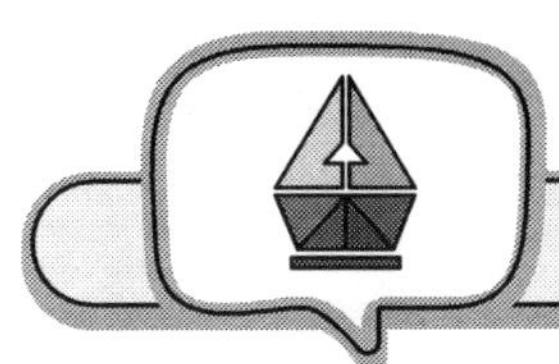

Mastering this skill helps you:

- Approach vocabulary questions methodically rather than relying on first impressions.
- Recognize when a familiar word is being used in a specialized or uncommon way.
- Eliminate incorrect answer choices with greater confidence.
- Transfer these analytical skills to other reading tasks beyond standardized tests.

Types of Vocabulary-in-Context Questions

Standardized tests typically present vocabulary questions in predictable formats. Understanding these patterns helps you recognize what the question is really asking.

Example 1: Standard Vocabulary-in-Context Format

In a typical vocabulary-in-context question, you'll see something like:

"As used in line 24, the word 'conductor' most nearly means..."

The question will be followed by four answer choices that present different definitions of the word. Your task is to determine which meaning matches how the word is used in the passage.

Let's look at how this works with an actual test-style passage:

Passage excerpt: "Prior to Edison's innovations, electricity remained largely a scientific curiosity rather than a practical power source. While many researchers explored its properties, few envisioned its potential as a universal conductor of light and information. Edison's laboratory experiments transformed theoretical knowledge into practical applications that would eventually illuminate homes worldwide."

Question: As used in line 3, "conductor" most nearly means: A) a person who directs an orchestra, B) a substance that transmits heat or electricity, C) a person who collects tickets on a train, D) a channel or medium for conveying something

To answer this question correctly, you need to:

1. Return to the passage and find the word in context
2. Analyze how it's being used in that specific sentence
3. Substitute each answer choice to see which one makes sense

In this example, the context talks about electricity's potential "as a universal conductor of light and information." Looking at the answer choices, B might seem right because it mentions electricity, but that's a trap. The passage is using "conductor" to mean a channel or medium for transmitting something (in this case, light and information), making D the correct answer.

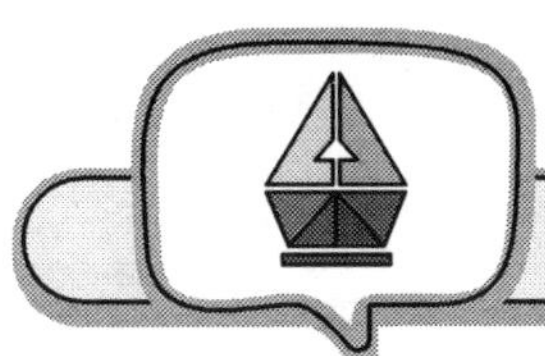

Example 2: Multiple-Meaning Words in Context

Many vocabulary questions focus on common words with multiple meanings. The key is determining which specific meaning applies in the passage.

Passage excerpt: "The archaeologist's pioneering research challenged conventional narratives about Aztec civilization. Though initially met with resistance from established scholars, her findings gradually gained currency as new excavations yielded corroborating evidence. Her reinterpretation of ceremonial artifacts cast ancient practices in a new light, illuminating the sophisticated astronomical knowledge that informed Aztec religious observances."

Question: In line 2, the word "resistance" most nearly means: A) electrical impedance B) physical strength training C) opposition or refusal D) immunity to disease

In this case, "resistance" is used to describe how established scholars responded to new research. While you might be familiar with resistance in electrical contexts (A) or exercise (B), the context clearly indicates that meaning C (opposition or refusal) is correct. The scholars were opposing or refusing to accept the new research.

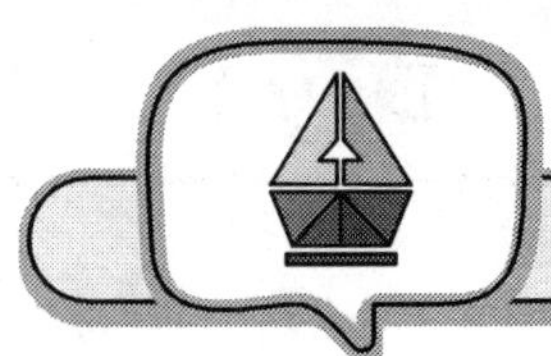

Vocabulary in SAT-Style Reading

Directions: Read the following passage and then answer the questions that follow.

"The Astronomical Achievements of the Aztec Civilization"

The Aztec civilization, which flourished in central Mexico from the 14th to the 16th centuries, developed sophisticated systems for understanding celestial movements that rivaled contemporary European astronomical knowledge. Contrary to persistent misconceptions that characterize pre-Columbian societies as primitive, archaeological evidence reveals that Aztec astronomers maintained meticulous observations of celestial bodies and integrated this knowledge into both their calendar systems and architectural designs.

The Aztec calendar stone, often erroneously called the "Aztec Calendar," actually represents not merely a timekeeping device but a complex cosmological model. This monumental sculpture embodies their cyclical conception of time and space, with the central deity Tonatiuh surrounded by symbols representing both temporal cycles and cardinal directions. While European astronomy was advancing toward heliocentric models, Aztec cosmology approached celestial observation through a distinct conceptual framework that nevertheless achieved remarkable predictive accuracy.

Aztec astronomical knowledge directly informed agricultural practices, religious ceremonies, and imperial administration. Their calendar system, consisting of a 260-day ritual cycle that meshed with a 365-day solar calendar, regulated planting schedules with precision that ensured agricultural productivity. Temple alignments in Tenochtitlan correspond to significant astronomical events, particularly solstices and equinoxes, demonstrating how celestial knowledge was literally built into the fabric of Aztec urban environments.

The Spanish conquest, unfortunately, arrested the independent development of Aztec astronomy. Early colonial accounts often dismissed indigenous knowledge systems as superstition, while systematic destruction of codices eliminated many primary records of Aztec astronomical observations. This cultural disruption means that contemporary understanding of Aztec astronomical achievements remains partial, reconstructed through surviving monuments, archaeological evidence, and the fragmented accounts preserved in post-conquest documents.

Recent scholarship has begun to appreciate the empirical foundations of Aztec astronomy, recognizing that their celestial observations reflected centuries of systematic study rather than merely religious speculation. This revised understanding challenges Eurocentric narratives about scientific development and invites consideration of how different cultural frameworks can produce valid systems of natural knowledge through distinct methodological approaches.

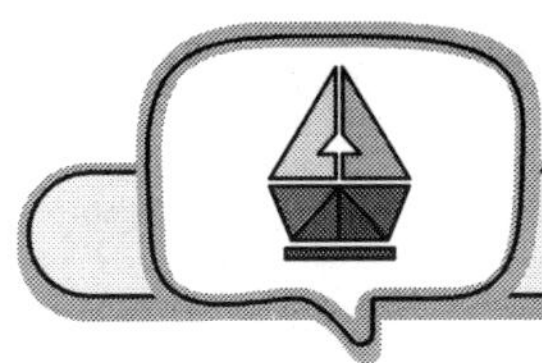

Week 4 • Practice Activity 1

Question 1: As used in line 3, “rivaled” most nearly means:

A. competed against

B. fought with

C. equaled in quality

D. threatened the existence of

Question 2: As used in line 3, “persistent” most nearly means:

A. determined

B. continuing to exist

C. insistent

D. recurring

Question 3: As used in line 15, “informed” most nearly means:

A. notified

B. educated

C. informed

D. influenced or shaped

Question 4: As used in line 26, “partial” most nearly means:

A. incomplete

B. biased

C. favoring

D. existing only in part

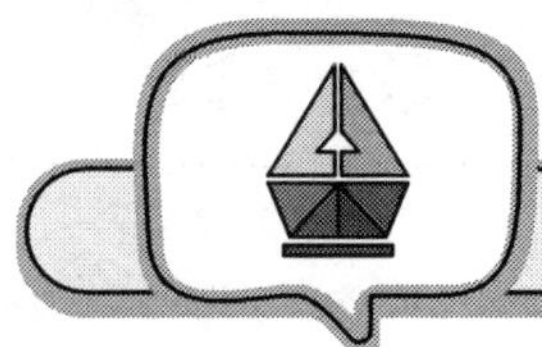

Key Concept #2: Applying Context Analysis Strategies

Why It Matters

Vocabulary-in-context questions require a systematic approach rather than relying on your first impression of a word's meaning. Even if you think you know a word, test-makers often select passages where common words are used in less familiar ways. Developing a step-by-step strategy ensures you'll consider the actual context rather than jumping to conclusions.

Mastering this skill helps you:

- Avoid the trap of selecting a familiar definition without checking the context.
- Break down complex sentences to understand how words function within them.
- Use contextual clues effectively to determine meaning.
- Apply elimination strategies when you're unsure about the correct answer.

Step-by-Step Context Analysis

When approaching vocabulary-in-context questions, follow these steps to ensure you're considering how the word functions in that specific passage.

Example 3: Context Analysis Process

Let's walk through the process using a test-style example:

Passage excerpt: "Though the jungle expedition proved physically taxing, Dr. Rivera found the experience intellectually exhilarating. Each day brought new botanical specimens that challenged existing classification systems. Despite the primitive conditions of the field camp, she maintained meticulous records, determined that her observations should not be compromised by environmental hardships."

Question: As used in line 3, "primitive" most nearly means: A) ancient or prehistoric, B) basic or rudimentary, C) original or primary, D) uncivilized or barbaric

- **Step 1:** Return to the passage and read the sentence containing the word. "Despite the primitive conditions of the field camp, she maintained meticulous records..."
- **Step 2:** Form your own definition before looking at answer choices. In this context, "primitive" seems to describe the basic, simple, or lacking-in-modern-amenities nature of the camp.
- **Step 3:** Try substituting each answer choice in the original sentence. A) "Despite the ancient conditions..." - Doesn't make sense; conditions aren't old. B) "Despite the basic conditions..." - Makes sense; camp lacks advanced facilities. C) "Despite the original conditions..." - Doesn't fit the context. D) "Despite the uncivilized conditions..." - Possible but too extreme for describing a field camp.
- **Step 4:** Select the best match. Answer B (basic or rudimentary) best matches how "primitive" is used in this context.

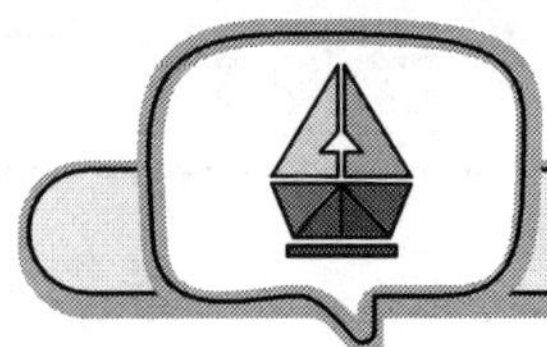

Example 4: Using Surrounding Context Clues

Sometimes you need to look beyond the immediate sentence to find clues about a word's meaning.

Passage excerpt: "Many climate scientists argue that current environmental policies remain nominal in addressing the scale of global challenges. While governments publicly commit to emissions targets, actual implementation measures often lack the substance necessary to achieve these goals. This disparity between stated ambitions and tangible actions has led to increasing skepticism among environmental advocates."

Question: As used in line 2, "nominal" most nearly means: A) relating to names, B) existing in name only; not real or substantial, C) very small in amount, D) related to currency or money

- **Step 1:** Read the sentence with the target word. "Many climate scientists argue that current environmental policies remain nominal in addressing the scale of global challenges."
- **Step 2:** Look for clarifying context in surrounding sentences. The next sentence mentions a "disparity between stated ambitions and tangible actions" and policies that "lack the substance necessary," suggesting the policies exist in name but not in substantial effect.
- **Step 3:** Form your own definition. Based on the context, "nominal" seems to mean existing in name only, without real substance.
- **Step 4:** Check answer choices. Answer B (existing in name only; not real or substantial) matches the contextual meaning.

Multiple-Meaning Words

Directions: Read each sentence and then answer the question that follows.

Sentence 1: The climatology team will conduct a series of double-blind trials to validate their working model of atmospheric carbon cycling.

Question 1: What does "conduct" most likely mean in this context?

A. to direct or lead an organized activity or process

B. to allow heat or electricity to pass through

C. to behave in a particular manner

D. to guide someone along a path or route

Sentence 2: During closing arguments, the defense attorney strategically addressed apparent contradictions in the timeline of events.

Question 2: What does "addressed" most likely mean in this context?

A. to mail a letter to a specific location

B. to formally speak to an audience

C. to confront or deal with a problem or issue

D. to describe someone's place of residence

Sentence 3: The illuminated manuscript from the 14th century illuminated cultural rituals and social norms often overlooked by historians.

Question 3: What does "illuminated" most likely mean in this context?

A. to physically brighten or make visible with light

B. to decorate a text with gold leaf or detailed illustrations

C. to celebrate something with fireworks or light displays

D. to make intellectually or conceptually clear

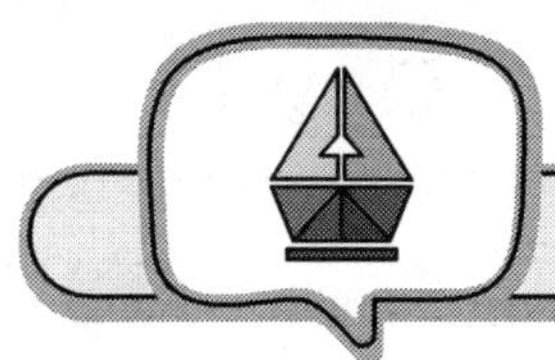

Week 4 • Practice Activity 2

Sentence 4: The delegates of the constitutional convention will draft a revised charter that reflects current institutional goals.

Question 4: What does "draft" most likely mean in this context?

A. a current of air entering a room

B. a preliminary version of a written document

C. a selection process for military service

D. a portion of beer drawn from a keg

Sentence 5: In an effort to track biodiversity loss, marine biologists regularly monitor fluctuations in coral reef health using satellite imaging and diver observations.

Question 5: What does "monitor" most likely mean in this context?

A. a person who supervises students

B. a screen used to display computer output

C. to observe and check systematically over time

D. a type of large tropical lizard

Sentence 6: Before entering foreign markets, the company must secure additional venture capital to ensure a stable launch.

Question 6: What does "secure" most likely mean in this context?

A. to fasten or lock something to prevent movement

B. to obtain or acquire something, often through effort

C. to protect someone from harm or danger

D. to ensure a safe internet connection

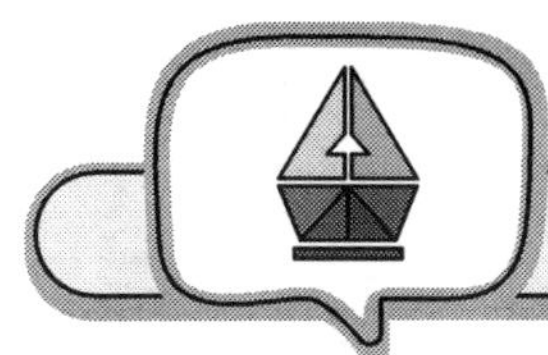

Sentence 7: Her aptitude for abstract reasoning allowed her to detect underlying patterns that others overlooked entirely.

Question 7: What does "abstract" most likely mean in this context?

A. a summary of a research paper

B. a painting without realistic representation

C. theoretical or conceptual rather than concrete

D. to physically remove or separate something

Sentence 8: The documentary series will feature firsthand interviews with climatologists who have conducted field research in the Arctic.

Question 8: What does "feature" most likely mean in this context?

A. to give special prominence to something or someone

B. a part of the face, like the eyes or the nose

C. a full-length film shown in a theater

D. a physical characteristic of a product

Well done! Tomorrow, we'll explore strategies for dealing with unfamiliar words on standardized tests.

Developing Strategies for Unfamiliar Words

By the end of this lesson, you'll be able to:

- Apply word part analysis to determine the meaning of unfamiliar terms.
- Use context clues effectively when encountering unknown vocabulary.
- Recognize word families to expand your understanding of related terms.
- Develop inference skills for vocabulary challenges on standardized tests.

Key Concept #1: Word Part Analysis for Test Success

Why It Matters

Even strong readers encounter unfamiliar words on standardized tests. When this happens, breaking down words into their component parts—roots, prefixes, and suffixes—can help you make educated guesses about meaning. This strategy is particularly valuable on timed tests when you can't stop to look up definitions.

Mastering this skill helps you:

- Decode unfamiliar vocabulary without external references.
- Recognize patterns in word formation across multiple terms.
- Make educated guesses when exact definitions aren't known.
- Build your vocabulary more efficiently by understanding word formation patterns.

Root Analysis for Unfamiliar Words

The ability to identify and understand common word roots dramatically increases your vocabulary power on standardized tests.

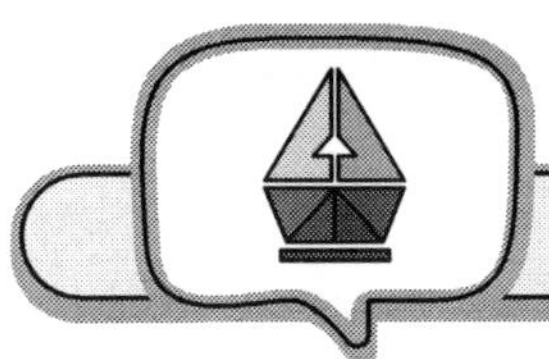

Example 1: Root Analysis in Test Passages

Standardized test passages often include academic or specialized vocabulary. Breaking these words into their component parts can help you determine their meanings.

Science passage excerpt: "The bioluminescent organisms in deep ocean environments have evolved photophores—specialized light-producing organs that serve multiple functions. These structures can attract prey, confuse predators, or facilitate intraspecies communication. The photogenic cells within these organs contain luciferin, which produces light through oxidation."

In this passage, even without prior knowledge, you can determine the meanings of specialized terms through root analysis:

- **Bio/lumin/escent**: bio (life) + lumin (light) + escent (becoming) = becoming light from living things
- **Photo/phores**: photo (light) + phore (bearer/carrier) = structures that carry or produce light
- **Intra/species**: intra (within) + species = within the same species
- **Photo/genic**: photo (light) + genic (producing) = light-producing
- **Luci/ferin**: luci (light) + ferin (related to carrying) = substance that carries or produces light

By recognizing these common roots, you can understand the passage's specialized vocabulary without needing to know these exact terms beforehand.

Example 2: Prefixes and Suffixes in Test Context

Prefixes and suffixes modify root meanings in predictable ways. Recognizing these patterns helps you navigate vocabulary in test passages.

History passage excerpt: "The postcolonial period witnessed unprecedented demographic shifts as newly independent nations established governance structures. Many countries faced the challenge of reconciling preexisting tribal boundaries with arbitrary territorial demarcations imposed during colonial rule. This mismatch often led to interethnic tensions that destabilized fledgling governments."

Analyzing word parts in this passage:

- **Post/colonial**: post (after) + colonial = after colonial rule
- **Un/precedent/ed**: un (not) + precedent (previous example) + ed (past tense) = never happened before
- **Pre/exist/ing**: pre (before) + exist + ing = having existed before
- **De/marc/ations**: de (completely) + marc (mark) + ations (process/state) = process of marking boundaries
- **Inter/ethnic**: inter (between) + ethnic = between different ethnic groups
- **De/stabil/ized**: de (reversal) + stabil (stable) + ized (caused to be) = caused to become unstable

These affixes follow consistent patterns that can help you determine meanings even when the complete word is unfamiliar.

Root Analysis in ACT-Style Science Reading

Directions: Read the following passage and then answer the questions that follow.

"Adaptive Mechanisms in Saharan Ecosystems"

The Sahara Desert presents one of Earth's most challenging environments for biological organisms. Extreme aridity, temperature fluctuations, and nutrient-poor soils create conditions that would be uninhabitable for most species. However, remarkable adaptations have evolved among the desert's flora and fauna that demonstrate the resilience of life even in seemingly inhospitable settings.

Desert plants exhibit multiple xeromorphic traits that enable survival during extended drought periods. Many species have developed extensive root systems that can access groundwater sources far below the surface. Others display crassulacean acid metabolism, a photosynthetic adaptation that allows stomata to remain closed during hot daylight hours, significantly reducing water loss while still permitting carbon fixation. The waxy cuticles and reduced leaf surface area characteristic of desert vegetation further minimize transpiration in these moisture-limited environments.

Animal species demonstrate equally impressive thermoregulatory adaptations. Many desert mammals are nocturnal, avoiding daytime heat through behavioral modification. Fossorial species escape extreme surface temperatures by remaining in underground burrows during peak heat. Physiological adaptations include efficient water conservation mechanisms such as highly concentrated urine and dry feces. The desert jerboa exemplifies these adaptations with its remarkable osmoregulatory capacity, requiring no free-standing water throughout its lifespan.

What appears to the casual observer as a barren landscape actually supports complex ecological interactions. Ephemeral plant communities emerge rapidly after rare precipitation events, completing their entire life cycles before conditions become desiccated again. These brief periods of productivity create resource pulses that sustain granivorous and insectivorous consumer populations throughout extended dry periods.

Recent research suggests that Saharan ecosystems may be particularly vulnerable to anthropogenic climate alterations. As global temperatures increase, already extreme conditions may exceed physiological thresholds for even the most highly adapted desert specialists. Understanding these remarkable adaptations not only illuminates evolutionary processes but may provide insights for conservation strategies in an increasingly water-stressed world.

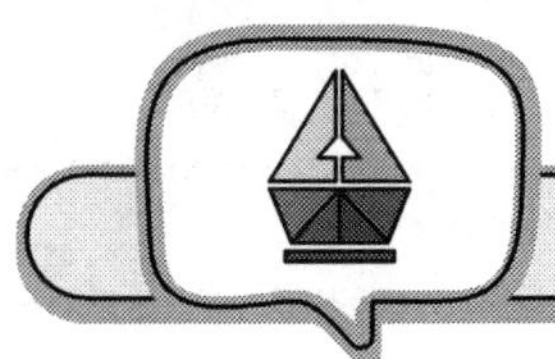

Week 4 • Practice Activity 1

Question 1: In the passage above, what is the meaning of "xeromorphic"?

A. related to dry conditions

B. growing slowly

C. heat-resistant

D. water-storing

Question 2: In the passage above, what is the meaning of "thermoregulatory"?

A. movement regulation

B. heat regulation

C. energy production

D. growth controls

Question 3: In the passage above, what is the meaning of "fossorial"?

A. related to fossils

B. adapted for digging

C. sunlight-avoiding

D. water-conserving

Question 4: In the passage above, what is the meaning of "desiccated"?

A. completely dried out

B. nutrient-depleted

C. sun-damaged

D. wind-eroded

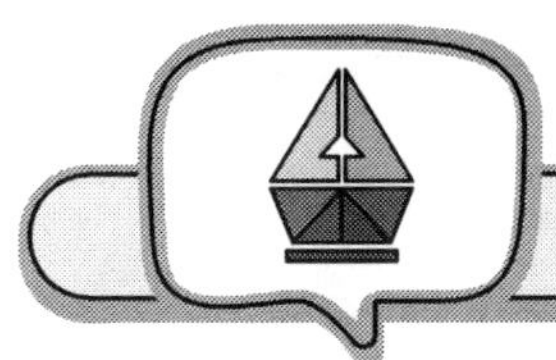

Key Concept #2: Context Clues in Standardized Tests

Why It Matters

Test passages often provide context clues that can help you determine the meaning of unfamiliar words. Learning to identify and use these clues efficiently is essential for success on timed tests, where you need to make quick but accurate decisions about vocabulary meaning.

Mastering this skill helps you:

- Identify different types of context clues in test passages.
- Use surrounding information to make educated guesses about word meanings.
- Approach unfamiliar vocabulary methodically rather than skipping it.
- Build confidence in handling challenging texts under test conditions.

Using Context Effectively on Tests

Test passages often include built-in clues to help readers understand specialized or unusual vocabulary. Learning to spot these clues helps you tackle unfamiliar words confidently.

Example 3: Definition and Explanation Clues

Test passages often include direct definitions or explanations of potentially unfamiliar terms.

Passage excerpt: "Many species exhibit mutualism, a symbiotic relationship in which both organisms benefit from their interaction. For example, pollinators receive nectar while plants achieve reproduction through pollen transfer. Unlike parasitism, where one organism benefits at another's expense, mutualistic relationships contribute to the fitness of both participants."

In this passage, several context clues help define unfamiliar terms:

- "Mutualism" is directly defined as "a symbiotic relationship in which both organisms benefit."
- An example clarifies this definition (pollinators and plants).
- A contrast with "parasitism" further clarifies by showing what mutualism is not.
- The final sentence reinforces the key characteristic of mutual benefit.

Even without prior knowledge of these ecological terms, you can determine their meanings from the context provided.

Example 4: Inference Clues for Vocabulary

Sometimes context requires more inference to determine word meanings, requiring you to connect information across sentences.

Passage excerpt: "The author's terse writing style presented challenges for readers accustomed to Victorian prose. Her sentences rarely exceeded ten words, and she eschewed elaborate descriptions in favor of stark dialogue. This minimalist approach initially alienated critics, who mistook brevity for simplicity rather than recognizing the meticulous craft underlying her concise expression."

While "terse" isn't directly defined, multiple context clues help determine its meaning:

- The contrast with "Victorian prose" (known for being elaborate and lengthy)
- The reference to short sentences ("rarely exceeded ten words")
- The mention of "eschewed elaborate descriptions" (avoiding lengthy descriptions)
- The terms "brevity" and "concise" later in the passage
- The overall characterization of a "minimalist approach"

From these clues, you can infer that "terse" means using few words, brief, or concise—even if you've never encountered the word before.

Week 4 • Practice Activity 2

Context Clues for Unfamiliar Words

Directions: For each sentence or passage below, use context clues to determine the meaning of the bolded word.

1. The speaker's **loquacious** nature made what should have been a brief presentation last over two hours, as she seemed unable to express any idea concisely or stick to her main points.

Meaning: ....

....

2. Unlike her **gregarious** brother, who thrived at parties and social gatherings, Tia preferred quiet evenings with one or two close friends, finding large crowds emotionally draining.

Meaning: ....

....

3. The archaeological site had remained **pristine** for centuries, untouched by looters or previous excavations, giving researchers a rare opportunity to study an undisturbed ancient settlement.

Meaning: ....

....

4. The coach praised the young athlete's **tenacity**. Despite facing multiple setbacks throughout the season, including a minor injury and several close losses, she never considered quitting and continued to train with unwavering determination.

Meaning: ....

....

5. The debate quickly became **acrimonious**, with both participants abandoning reasoned arguments in favor of personal attacks and increasingly hostile remarks that created a tense atmosphere in the auditorium.

Meaning: ....

....

Key Concept #3: Word Families and Vocabulary Expansion

Why It Matters

Words often appear in families with related meanings but different parts of speech or slight variations in meaning. Recognizing these relationships helps you understand unfamiliar words by connecting them to terms you already know. This knowledge allows you to expand your effective vocabulary quickly during test preparation.

Mastering this skill helps you:

- Connect unfamiliar words to known terms within the same word family.
- Recognize how different suffixes change a word's part of speech.
- Expand your vocabulary by learning patterns rather than isolated words.
- Apply knowledge of one word to understand related terms in test passages.

Word Family Recognition

Understanding how words connect within families allows you to leverage knowledge of one word to understand related terms.

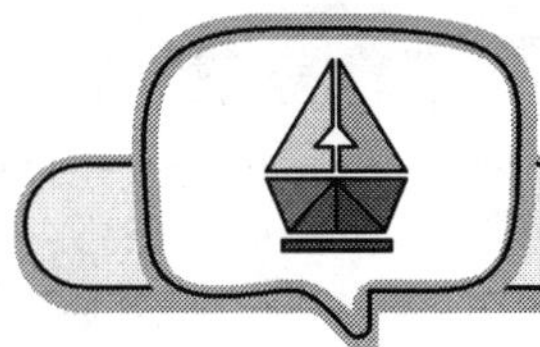

Example 5: Word Families in Test Passages

Test passages often include multiple words from the same family, allowing you to use familiar terms to understand unfamiliar ones.

Passage excerpt: "The proliferation of digital technology has transformed how information circulates in society. What once required physical proximity now proliferates instantly across global networks. This rapid proliferative capacity creates both opportunities and challenges for institutions that previously controlled information flow."

In this passage, different forms of the same word appear:

- **Proliferation** (noun): the rapid increase or spread of something
- **Proliferates** (verb): spreads rapidly or multiplies
- **Proliferative** (adjective): tending to increase rapidly or spread

Even if you know only one of these forms, you can use that knowledge to understand the others by recognizing the shared root and how different suffixes change the part of speech.

Example 6: Leveraging Word Families

Recognizing word families helps you maximize your existing vocabulary knowledge.

SAT-style question: As used in line 8, "mitigate" most nearly means: A) cause, B) lessen, C) increase, D) investigate

Even if you're unfamiliar with "mitigate," you might know related words in its family:

- **Mitigation**: the act of reducing the severity of something
- **Mitigating** (as in "mitigating factors"): factors that make something less severe
- **Mitigated**: made less severe or intense

Using this word family knowledge, you can determine that "mitigate" means to lessen or reduce the severity of something (answer B).

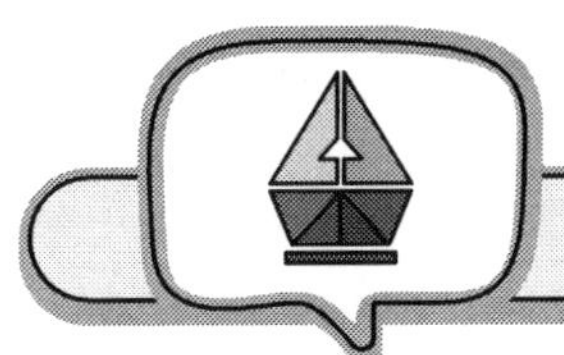

Mastering Word Families in Context

Directions: Read each excerpt below and answer the following question.

Excerpt 1: In many democratic societies, legislation is not simply imposed—it evolves through public discourse and committee debate. Lawmakers may legislate new policies in response to emerging social challenges, but without legitimacy, even well-crafted laws can be contested.

Question 1: Based on the passage, what is the most accurate meaning of legitimize?

A. to prohibit something through legal action

B. to question the fairness of a law

C. to make something lawful or accepted

D. to replace outdated legislation

Excerpt 1: The architect's design was praised for its originality, but the conception of the project began years earlier. As the team conceived of ways to blend sustainability with aesthetic appeal, they encountered numerous obstacles. Yet, the final structure reflected a clear and powerful concept.

Question 2: What does the word inconceivable most likely mean in academic or professional writing?

A. difficult to measure with precision

B. impossible to imagine or believe

C. related to visual design or planning

D. based on philosophical ideals

Excerpt 3: Despite facing repeated setbacks, the researchers demonstrated remarkable persistence. Their persistent efforts eventually yielded promising data, showing that viral resistance may persist even under new drug protocols.

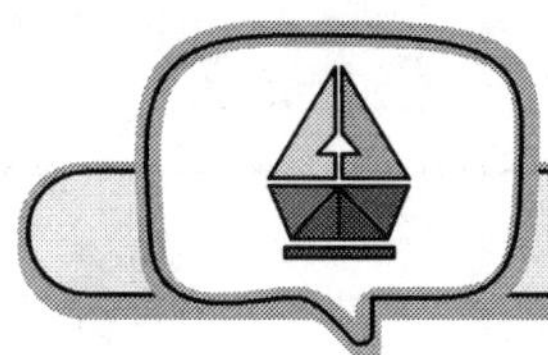

Week 4 • Practice Activity 3

Question 3: Which of the following is the best definition of persistence in this scientific context?

A. the ongoing presence or endurance of something over time

B. the tendency to fade or weaken over time

C. a repeated attempt to overcome small obstacles

D. a conscious decision to ignore negative results

Excerpt 4: Each participant was expected to contribute a section to the group project. The professor emphasized that the contributions should be original and well-researched. One student raised a concern that such pressure could feel contributory to academic burnout.

Question 4: What is the most precise meaning of contributory in the final sentence?

A. preventing or alleviating a problem

B. irrelevant to the main topic

C. receiving recognition or credit

D. causing or helping to cause something

Excerpt 5: Before implementing the policy, the city council conducted an evaluation of its projected impact. The mayor stressed the need to re-evaluate annually, given how quickly conditions shift. Citizens were invited to submit feedback using an evaluative rubric developed by independent consultants.

Question 5: Based on this passage, what does evaluative most likely mean?

A. designed to collect personal opinions

B. intended to guide fair and systematic judgment

C. written in formal or academic language

D. used only in business or finance settings

Great job! Tomorrow, we'll apply these strategies to test-like practice questions.

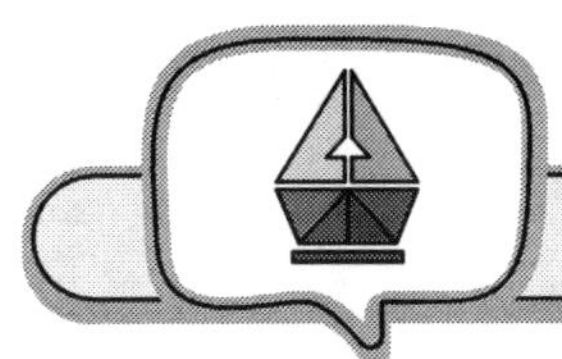

Practicing Vocabulary Application in Tests

By the end of this lesson, you'll be able to:

- Apply vocabulary strategies under test-like conditions.
- Identify and avoid common vocabulary question traps.
- Combine multiple strategies to tackle challenging questions.
- Develop efficient approaches for vocabulary questions during timed tests.

Key Concept #1: Test-Taking Strategies for Vocabulary Questions

Why It Matters

Knowing vocabulary strategies is important, but applying them effectively under test conditions requires practice and specific techniques. Time pressure, test anxiety, and the structure of standardized tests create additional challenges beyond simply knowing word meanings. Learning to approach vocabulary questions strategically helps you maximize your performance even when facing unfamiliar terms.

Mastering this skill helps you:

- Approach vocabulary questions systematically rather than randomly.
- Manage your time effectively during vocabulary sections.
- Avoid common mistakes that test-makers expect students to make.
- Make educated guesses when you're unsure of the exact meaning.

Effective Test-Taking Approaches

Standardized tests like the SAT and ACT require specific strategies for vocabulary questions. Here are the key approaches that will help you succeed:

1. **Read the entire sentence or paragraph containing the word.** Don't just focus on the single sentence with the target word. Often, the meaning becomes clear only when you understand the broader discussion.

2. **Form your own definition before looking at answer choices.** This prevents you from being swayed by tempting but incorrect options.

3. **Use the process of elimination.** Even if you don't know the exact definition, you can often eliminate answers that clearly don't fit the context.

4. **Watch for signal words that indicate relationships.** Terms like "however," "similarly," "in contrast," and "moreover" show how ideas connect and can help clarify meaning.

5. **Look for synonyms and definition clues in the surrounding text.** Authors often provide synonyms or explanations for potentially unfamiliar terms.

6. **Substitute each answer choice into the original sentence.** This can help you determine which meaning fits most naturally in context.

7. **Pay attention to tone and attitude.** The author's perspective can help you determine whether a word has positive, negative, or neutral connotations.

8. **Don't spend too much time on any single vocabulary question.** If you're stuck, mark it and return after answering other questions.

9. **Always make an educated guess.** There's no penalty for wrong answers on the SAT or ACT, so never leave a question blank.

10. **Trust the context over your prior knowledge.** Common words often have specific meanings in particular contexts that differ from everyday usage.

Example 1: Process of Elimination Strategy

When facing challenging vocabulary questions, elimination can be your most powerful tool. Even if you're not immediately sure of the correct answer, you can often identify clearly wrong options.

Test question: As used in line 17, "endemic" most nearly means: A) widespread, B) threatening, C) native to a specific place, D) increasing rapidly

Elimination process:

1. Return to the passage: "Unlike many waterborne illnesses that occur globally, this parasite is endemic to tropical regions with specific temperature and humidity conditions."
2. Analyze the context: The passage contrasts "globally" with "endemic to tropical regions," suggesting the word relates to geographic limitation.
3. Eliminate options:
   - ◇ Option A (widespread): Contradicts the contrast with "globally"
   - ◇ Option B (threatening): Nothing in context suggests danger or threat
   - ◇ Option D (increasing rapidly): No indication of growth or change rate
4. Select the remaining option: C (native to a specific place)

Even without knowing the exact definition of "endemic," the process of elimination leads to the correct answer (C). This strategy is particularly valuable for vocabulary questions because wrong answers often represent different meanings of the word that don't fit the specific context.

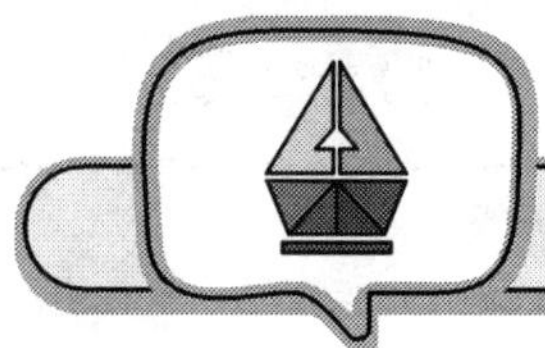

Example 2: Substituting Answer Choices in Context

One effective strategy is to substitute each answer choice back into the original sentence to see which one makes the most sense in context. This approach helps you test definitions in a concrete way.

Passage excerpt: "The research team's findings were anomalous, contradicting years of established theory and requiring scientists to reconsider fundamental principles in the field."

Question: As used in line 1, "anomalous" most nearly means: A) incorrect, B) preliminary, C) unusual or irregular, D) anticipated

Substitution strategy in action:

1. First, locate the word in the passage: "The research team's findings were anomalous..."
2. Now substitute each answer choice into the sentence:
    - ◇ "The research team's findings were [incorrect]..." Does this fit? Possibly, but the passage doesn't specifically say the findings were wrong, just that they contradicted expectations.
    - ◇ "The research team's findings were [preliminary]..." Does this fit? No, nothing suggests these are early or initial findings.
    - ◇ "The research team's findings were [unusual or irregular]..." Does this fit? Yes, this works well with "contradicting years of established theory," which suggests the findings were unexpected or out of the ordinary.
    - ◇ "The research team's findings were [anticipated]..." Does this fit? No, this contradicts the idea that the findings went against established theory.
3. By testing each option in context, we can determine that "unusual or irregular" (Option C) makes the most sense and maintains the logical flow of the passage.

This substitution strategy helps you directly test how each definition works in the actual context, making it easier to identify the correct meaning even when you're not completely familiar with the word.

Vocabulary Questions in Test Format

Directions: Read the following passage and answer the questions that follow.

"The Agricultural Revolution in Mesoamerica"

The domestication of maize in Mesoamerica represents one of humanity's most profound agricultural achievements, transforming nomadic populations into sedentary societies with complex social structures. Archaeological evidence suggests that this process began approximately 9,000 years ago in Mexico's Central Balsas River Valley, where indigenous peoples gradually modified teosinte, a wild grass bearing little resemblance to modern corn, through selective breeding. This protracted development ultimately yielded a staple crop that would sustain burgeoning civilizations throughout the Americas.

Unlike the relatively straightforward domestication of certain Old World grains, maize required extensive human intervention to become a viable food source. Early cultivators selected for larger cobs, increased kernel rows, and reduced protective kernel casings—modifications that rendered the plant entirely dependent on human cultivation for reproduction. This symbiotic relationship exemplifies the intricate coevolution of human societies and their domesticated species, each exerting selective pressure on the other's development.

The repercussions of maize agriculture extended far beyond dietary change. As communities established permanent settlements around reliable food production, social hierarchies emerged, with specialized roles replacing the egalitarian structures typical of hunter-gatherer groups. Surplus production enabled population growth and urbanization, creating the demographic foundation for Mesoamerican civilizations like the Olmec, Maya, and Aztec. The cultural significance of maize transcended mere sustenance, becoming integral to religious practices and cosmological beliefs throughout the region.

Recent genetic and isotopic analyses have refined our understanding of this agricultural revolution, revealing a more nuanced progression than previously theorized. Evidence now suggests that maize was initially cultivated not as a dietary staple but rather for producing ceremonial beverages, with its role as a primary food source developing gradually over millennia. This insight illuminates the complex interplay between cultural practices and subsistence strategies that characterized early agricultural societies.

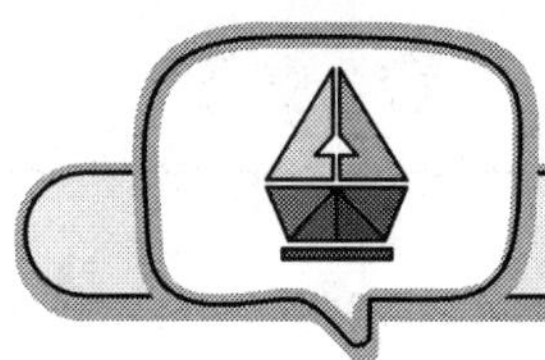

Week 4 • Practice Activity 1

Question 1: As used in line 2, "sedentary" most nearly means:

A. physically inactive

B. permanently settled

C. slowly developing

D. technologically advanced

Question 2: As used in line 6, "protracted" most nearly means:

A. planned

B. difficult

C. extended over time

D. successful

Question 3: As used in line 10, "viable" most nearly means:

A. financially valuable

B. visible to observers

C. genetically diverse

D. capable of success

Question 4: As used in line 21, "transcended" most nearly means:

A. exceeded or went beyond

B. changed gradually

C. connected spiritually

D. became essential to

Key Concept #2: Avoiding Common Vocabulary Question Traps

Why It Matters

Test-makers deliberately design vocabulary questions with predictable traps to distinguish between students who truly understand word meanings in context and those who have only superficial knowledge. Recognizing these common traps helps you avoid making mistakes even when questions are designed to be misleading.

Mastering this skill helps you:

- Identify deliberately misleading answer choices.
- Look beyond familiar definitions to find contextual meanings.
- Avoid selecting answers based on word associations rather than actual meanings.
- Maintain accuracy even on challenging vocabulary questions.

Common Vocabulary Question Traps

Standardized tests include several specific types of traps in vocabulary questions designed to trick students who aren't carefully analyzing the context. Here are the major traps to watch for:

1. **The Common Definition Trap:** The test offers the most familiar meaning of a word when the passage uses it in a less common way. For example, giving "bright" to mean "intelligent" when the passage uses it to mean "well-lit."
2. **The Word Association Trap:** Answer choices relate to the topic of the passage but don't match the actual meaning of the word. For instance, if a passage discusses ocean life, a question about "current" might offer water-related definitions even if the word is being used to mean "present-day."
3. **The Synonym Swap Trap:** The test offers a synonym for another word in the sentence, not the word being asked about.
4. **The Definition Fragments Trap:** Options that include part of the word's meaning but miss crucial aspects of how it's used in context.
5. **The Tone Mismatch Trap:** Choices that have the correct basic meaning but wrong connotations (positive when the context is negative, or formal when the context is casual).
6. **The "Sounds Similar" Trap:** Options based on words that sound like the target word but have different meanings.
7. **The Collocation Confusion Trap:** Definitions that might work with the word in some phrases but not in the specific phrase used in the passage.

Let's see how to recognize and avoid these traps:

Example 3: The "Common Definition" Trap

One of the most frequent traps is providing the most common definition of a word when the passage uses it in a less familiar way.

Passage excerpt: "The professor conducted a thorough review of recent research, examining methodological approaches and evaluating the validity of conclusions. Her critical assessment revealed several promising studies that warranted further investigation."

Question: As used in line 3, "critical" most nearly means: A) finding fault, B) crucial or important, C) analytical and evaluative, D) dangerously unstable

Many students might select option A, associating "critical" with criticizing or finding fault—its most common everyday usage. However, in academic contexts, "critical" often means "involving careful analysis and judgment," making C the correct answer. The context of "assessment" and "evaluating validity" supports this analytical meaning rather than a fault-finding one.

Example 4: The "Word Association" Trap

Another common trap involves answer choices that are associated with the target word but don't actually match its meaning in context.

Passage excerpt: "The expedition party found the terrain increasingly arduous as they ascended the mountain. What had begun as a manageable hike transformed into a grueling climb requiring technical equipment and specialized skills."

Question: As used in line 1, "arduous" most nearly means: A) mountainous, B) high-altitude, C) difficult and demanding, D) dangerous

Options A and B might tempt students because "arduous" appears in a sentence about mountain climbing, creating a word association. However, these choices reflect the setting, not the meaning of "arduous." The context indicates that the terrain became more challenging (option C), as reinforced by phrases like "grueling climb" and the need for technical equipment.

Trap Recognition

Directions: Read each sentence below and then answer the question that follows.,

Sentence 1: "The paleontologist's meticulous excavation techniques yielded fossils in remarkable condition, preserving delicate structures that might otherwise have been destroyed during extraction."

Question 1: As used in the passage, "meticulous" most nearly means:

A. slow
B. modern
C. scientific
D. extremely careful and precise

Sentence 2: "Though the author's first novel had been largely overlooked by critics, her sophomore effort garnered widespread acclaim for its innovative narrative structure and compelling characterization."

Question 2: As used in the passage, "garnered" most nearly means:

A. deserved
B. requested
C. received or collected
D. needed

Sentence 3: "The documentary presents a comprehensive examination of climate change, amalgamating scientific data, economic analysis, and personal narratives into a compelling call for action."

Question 3: As used in the passage, "amalgamating" most nearly means:

A. analyzing
B. combining or uniting
C. questioning
D. simplifying

Sentence 4: "The new urban development regulations stipulate minimum green space requirements for all construction projects exceeding one acre, with additional provisions for water conservation and native plantings."

Question 4: As used in the passage, "stipulate" most nearly means:

A. specify as a requirement
B. suggest
C. predict
D. prioritize

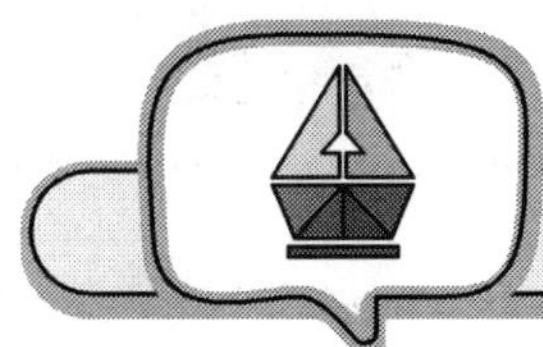

Key Concept #3: Integrating Multiple Vocabulary Strategies

Why It Matters

The most successful test-takers don't rely on just one approach for vocabulary questions. Instead, they combine multiple strategies—context analysis, word parts, elimination, and inferencing—to tackle even the most challenging questions. Learning to integrate these approaches provides you with a comprehensive toolkit for vocabulary success.

Mastering this skill helps you:

- Approach vocabulary questions flexibly rather than mechanically.
- Develop backup strategies when your initial approach doesn't yield a clear answer.
- Build confidence in handling unfamiliar vocabulary in various contexts.
- Improve your overall reading comprehension skills beyond vocabulary questions.

Combined Strategy Approach

When facing challenging vocabulary questions, using a single strategy might not be enough. Here's how to integrate multiple approaches for maximum effectiveness:

1. **Start with context analysis:** Always begin by examining how the word is used in the passage, looking at the surrounding sentences for clues about meaning.
2. **Apply word part knowledge:** If context isn't enough, analyze the word's roots, prefixes, and suffixes to determine possible meanings.
3. **Use elimination strategically:** Even with partial understanding, you can often rule out answers that clearly don't fit the context.
4. **Look for tone and connotation clues:** Consider whether the passage presents the concept positively, negatively, or neutrally.
5. **Check for definition patterns:** Many standardized tests repeat certain vocabulary words across different test versions, often using similar definitions.
6. **Use passage structure clues:** The organization of ideas in the passage (contrast, cause-effect, example) can clarify how the word functions.
7. **Apply subject matter knowledge:** Understanding the topic being discussed can help narrow down possible meanings.
8. **Consider word function:** Identify the word's part of speech (noun, verb, adjective) to eliminate definitions that don't match this function.

9. **Make strategic guesses:** When you're still uncertain after applying other strategies, make an educated guess based on the partial information you've gathered. This is especially important since there's no penalty for wrong answers on the SAT and ACT.

This integrated approach is particularly valuable when you encounter especially challenging vocabulary or when your initial strategy doesn't provide a clear answer.

Example 5: Multi-Strategy Analysis

Let's see how combining strategies works for a challenging vocabulary question:

Passage excerpt: "Although initially obdurate in his opposition to the proposal, the committee chair gradually became more receptive as colleagues presented compelling evidence of potential benefits. This evolution from rigid resistance to cautious consideration demonstrated the kind of intellectual flexibility essential for effective governance."

Question: As used in line 1, "obdurate" most nearly means:

A) angry B) confused C) stubborn and unyielding D) vocal

Combined strategy approach:

- **Context analysis:** The word describes the chair's initial "opposition" to a proposal, contrasted with later becoming "more receptive," suggesting a negative stance that changed.
- **Word part analysis:** "Obdurate" contains "dur-" (as in "durable" or "endure"), suggesting hardness or persistence.
- **Clarifying context:** The passage later refers to "rigid resistance" as part of the same behavior, providing a synonym clue.
- **Process of elimination:** Option A (angry): Opposition doesn't necessarily mean anger. Option B (confused): Nothing suggests confusion; the opposition seems deliberate. Option D (vocal): Being vocal describes how opposition is expressed, not its nature
- **Synthesis:** The context suggests someone who was firmly opposed and resistant to change (option C).

By combining multiple strategies, you can determine that "obdurate" means "stubborn and unyielding" (C) even if you've never encountered the word before.

Example 6: Strategic Guessing

Sometimes, despite your best efforts, you might still be uncertain about a vocabulary question. In such cases, strategic guessing using partial information can improve your odds significantly.

Passage excerpt: “The early photographs provide a glimpse into quotidian life during the Victorian era, capturing ordinary citizens engaged in commonplace activities rather than the formal portraits that dominated early photography.”

Question: As used in line 1, “quotidian” most nearly means: A) high-quality, B) everyday, C) forgotten, D) fascinating

Strategic guessing approach:

1. **Partial context analysis:** The passage mentions “ordinary citizens” and “commonplace activities” in connection with quotidian life.
2. **Contrasting context:** The passage contrasts these images with “formal portraits,” suggesting something informal or regular.
3. **Limited word part knowledge:** Even without knowing the root, you might recognize that “quot-” appears in words like “quote” and “quotation.”
4. **Educated elimination:**
    - ◇ The connection to “ordinary” and “commonplace” makes options A (high-quality) and D (fascinating) seem unlikely
    - ◇ Nothing suggests these aspects of life were “forgotten” (option C)
    - ◇ The parallel with “ordinary” and “commonplace” makes B (everyday) the most likely option

Even with incomplete information, strategic analysis can lead you to the correct answer (B). The word “quotidian” does indeed mean “everyday” or “occurring daily,” which matches the context clues about ordinary citizens and commonplace activities.

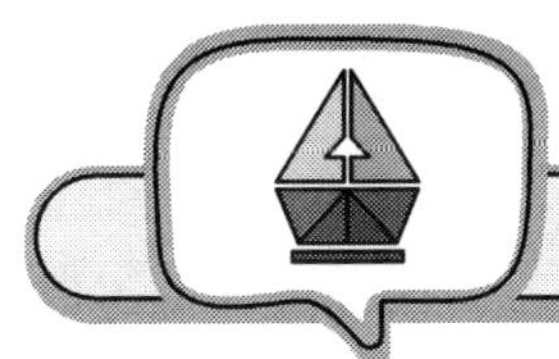

Applying Multiple Vocabulary Strategies

Directions: Read the following passage and then answer the questions that follow.

"Global Perspectives on Community and Identity"

The concept of "community" manifests differently across cultural contexts, reflecting diverse values and historical experiences. In many African societies, the philosophy of ubuntu—often summarized as "I am because we are"—creates a framework where individual identity remains inextricably linked to collective belonging. This perspective engenders social structures prioritizing communal harmony and intergenerational responsibility over personal ambition or achievement. Though sometimes romanticized by Western observers, these community-centered approaches offer viable alternatives to the atomized individualism characterizing many industrialized societies.

East Asian traditions similarly emphasize relational identity, though through distinct conceptual frameworks. The Japanese concept of amae describes a form of interdependence where individuals can presume upon others' benevolence within established relationships—a dynamic particularly salient in family and workplace hierarchies. This psychological orientation stands in stark contrast to Western valorization of self-reliance and autonomy. While critics might characterize such interdependence as constraining, proponents argue it fosters social cohesion and emotional security, often attenuated in more individualistic cultures.

Indigenous communities worldwide maintain yet other paradigms of belonging, frequently grounded in relationships not only with human collectives but also with ancestral spirits, non-human beings, and specific landscapes. The Australian Aboriginal concept of Country transcends Western notions of land ownership or even stewardship, representing instead a complex and reciprocal relationship where people belong to the land as much as land belongs to people. Such perspectives challenge conventional political and legal frameworks predicated on Enlightenment-derived notions of individual rights and property.

Globalization has precipitated unprecedented interactions between these diverse conceptualizations of community and identity. As migration patterns become increasingly fluid and digital technologies enable virtual communities transcending geographic boundaries, traditional demarcations between cultural paradigms grow increasingly permeable. This cross-fertilization generates both tension and innovation as communities negotiate between preserving distinctive cultural heritages and adapting to rapidly evolving social landscapes.

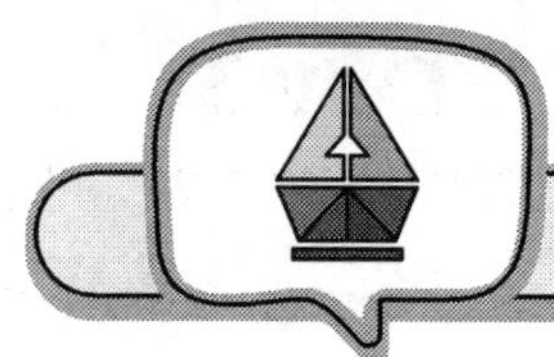

Week 4 • Practice Activity 3

Question 1: As used in line 5, "engenders" most nearly means:

A. confuses
B. gives birth to
C. creates or produces
D. improves

Question 2: As used in line 8, "atomized" most nearly means:

A. highly structured
B. broken into separate individuals
C. technologically advanced
D. logically analyzed

Question 3: As used in line 12, "salient" most nearly means:

A. positive
B. problematic
C. traditional
D. noticeable or prominent

Question 4: As used in line 16, "attenuated" most nearly means:

A. weakened or reduced
B. appreciated
C. required
D. examined

Question 5: As used in line 20, "transcends" most nearly means:

A. rejects or refuses
B. goes beyond or surpasses
C. perfectly illustrates
D. carefully preserves

Question 6: As used in line 25, "precipitated" most nearly means:

A. caused to happen quickly
B. fallen as rain
C. calculated accurately
D. avoided completely

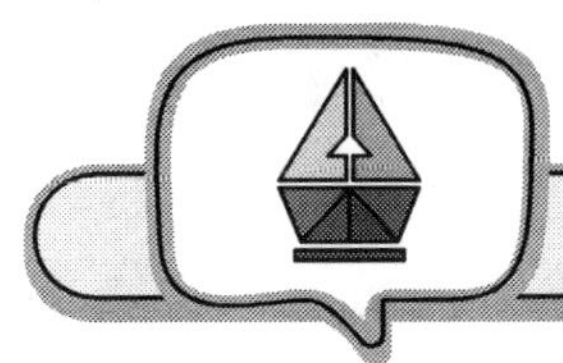

Week 4 • Final Reflection Questions

Directions: Take a few minutes to think about the lessons from this week, and then answer the questions below.

Question 1: Which strategy—context clues, word part analysis, or process of elimination—helped you most this week, and why do you think it worked well for you in timed conditions?

Question 2: How did this week's focus on multiple-meaning words challenge your assumptions about "easy" vocabulary?

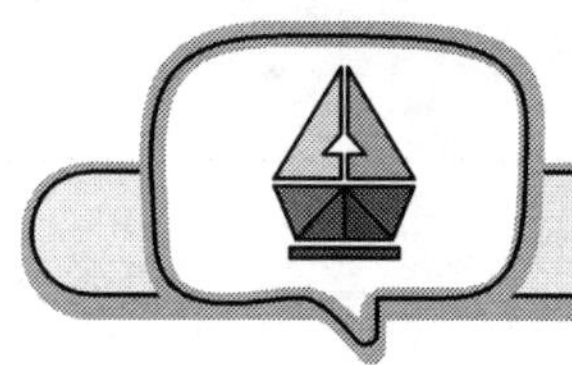

Week 4 • Final Reflection Questions

Great job! Next week, we will transition to author's purpose.

Final Thought

The vocabulary strategies you've learned this week are much more than test-taking tricks—they're powerful tools for becoming a more independent and confident reader. When you encounter unfamiliar words, you now have multiple approaches to unlock their meanings: analyzing context, breaking down word parts, recognizing relationships between words, and making educated inferences. These skills will serve you well beyond standardized tests, helping you tackle complex texts in all your classes and beyond. The most successful readers aren't necessarily those who know the most words initially, but those who have strategies for figuring out new words when they encounter them. You're now equipped with these strategies, ready to approach challenging vocabulary with confidence rather than frustration. As you continue preparing for the SAT or ACT, remember that every unfamiliar word is an opportunity to apply these skills—and with each application, your vocabulary and reading comprehension will continue to grow stronger.

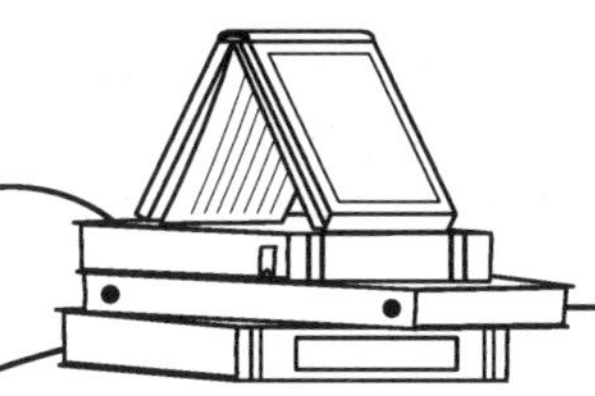

WEEK 5

Reading for Author's Purpose

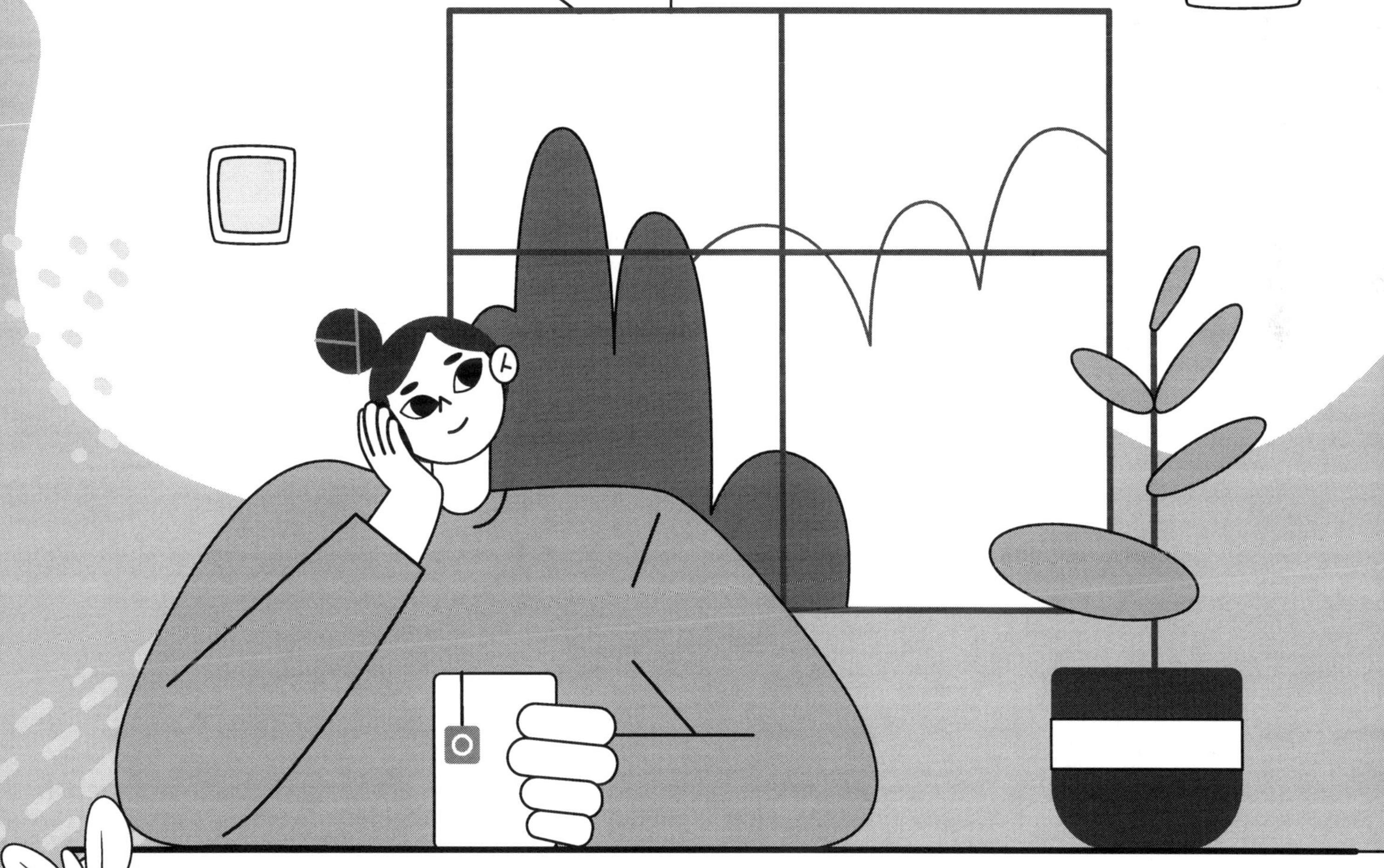

Identify explicit and implicit writing purposes and how they shape content and style. Learn to evaluate an author's effectiveness and understand how culture influences communication.

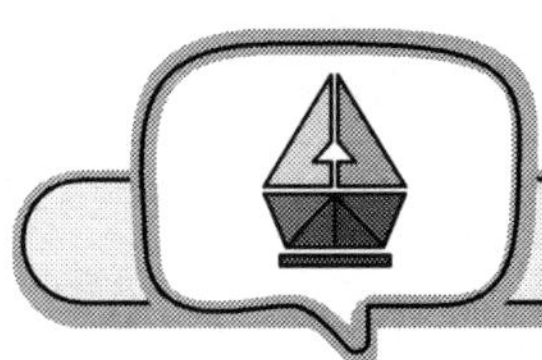

Week 5 • Reading for Author's Purpose

Introduction

This week, we'll explore one of the most powerful skills in reading comprehension: identifying and analyzing an author's purpose. Every text—whether it's a novel, research paper, speech, or advertisement—is created for a specific reason. Understanding why authors write what they write helps you interpret their messages more accurately and evaluate their effectiveness more critically. You'll learn to recognize both explicit statements of purpose and implicit clues that reveal an author's true intentions. By examining texts from diverse global perspectives, you'll also see how cultural context influences purpose. By the end of this week, you'll approach reading with a more analytical mindset, looking beyond what a text says to understand why it was written and how effectively it achieves its goals.

Identifying Explicit and Implicit Purposes

By the end of this lesson, you'll be able to:

- Distinguish between the basic purposes of informing, persuading, and entertaining.
- Identify explicit statements of purpose in different types of texts.
- Recognize implicit purpose through tone, word choice, and organizational patterns.
- Analyze how authors may combine multiple purposes within a single text.

Key Concept #1: Basic Categories of Author's Purpose

Why It Matters

Understanding an author's purpose provides a framework for interpreting everything in a text—from word choice to organization to use of evidence. When you know why someone is writing, you can better evaluate whether they've achieved their goals and whether their approach is appropriate for their audience. This awareness helps you become both a more perceptive reader and a more effective writer.

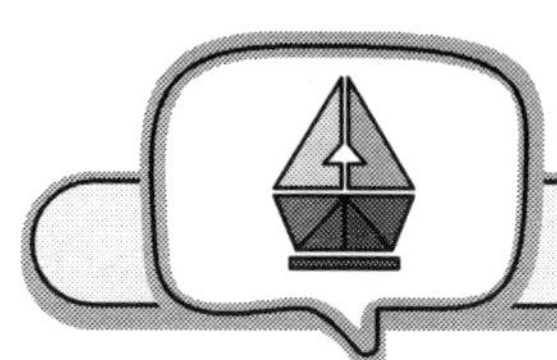

Week 5 • Reading for Author's Purpose

Mastering this skill helps you:

- Predict what types of information and techniques will appear in a text.
- Evaluate the effectiveness and appropriateness of an author's approach.
- Recognize when authors may have hidden or secondary purposes.
- Approach different types of texts with appropriate expectations.

The Primary Purposes of Writing

Authors generally write for one or more of three basic purposes: to inform, to persuade, or to entertain. Understanding these fundamental categories helps you establish a framework for analyzing texts.

- **To inform:** When authors write to inform, their primary goal is to provide accurate information, explain concepts, or increase understanding. These texts focus on facts, details, and clear explanations.
- **To persuade:** When authors write to persuade, they aim to change the reader's mind, influence beliefs, or motivate action. These texts include arguments, evidence, and persuasive techniques.
- **To entertain:** When authors write to entertain, they seek to engage readers through storytelling, humor, or creative expression. These texts prioritize reader engagement and emotional response.

However, many sophisticated texts combine these purposes. A historical novel might primarily entertain while also informing readers about a specific time period. A scientific article about climate change might inform readers about data while persuading them that action is needed. Learning to identify both primary and secondary purposes helps you understand texts in their full complexity.

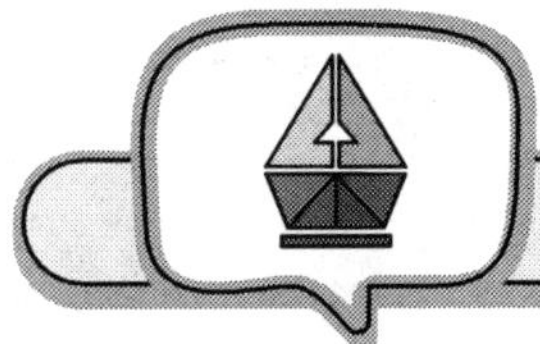

Example 1: Identifying Primary Purpose in Different Text Types

Let's examine how to identify the primary purpose in different types of texts:

News Article: This article opens with details about the unprecedented formation of three major hurricanes at once, provides data about wind speeds and projected paths, and quotes meteorologists explaining the unusual weather pattern.

The primary purpose is to inform. Key indicators include:

- Focus on factual information (dates, measurements, statistics)
- Neutral presentation of information without attempting to persuade
- Quotes from experts providing explanations rather than opinions
- Absence of emotional appeals or calls to action

Opinion Column: This piece begins by describing recent hurricane damage, argues that current emergency systems are inadequate, proposes specific policy changes, and urges readers to contact their representatives.

The primary purpose is to persuade. Key indicators include:

- Presents a clear position (current systems need to change)
- Uses evidence specifically to support this position
- Includes direct calls to action
- Uses emotional language to emphasize urgency

Short Story: This narrative follows a family preparing for an approaching hurricane, depicts their emotions and conflicts as they decide whether to evacuate, and creates tension through vivid descriptions of the worsening weather.

The primary purpose is to entertain. Key indicators include:

- Focus on characters and their experiences
- Dramatic narrative structure building to a climax
- Vivid sensory details to engage the reader
- Emphasis on emotional impact rather than factual information

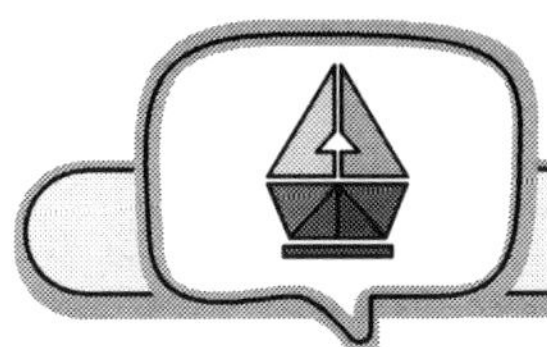

Example 2: Recognizing Combined Purposes

Many sophisticated texts blend multiple purposes. Consider this excerpt from a feature article about climate change in Pacific island nations:

"As dawn breaks over Kiribati, Teueroa Kitara wades into water that now covers what was once her family's garden. 'My grandparents grew taro here,' she explains, pointing to submerged plants struggling in the increasingly saline soil. 'Now we can only grow it in raised containers.' According to the Pacific Climate Change Science Program, sea levels in this region have risen at nearly three times the global average rate since 1993. Without significant global emissions reductions, scientists project that large portions of Kiribati may become uninhabitable within decades, forcing the displacement of communities that have existed here for thousands of years."

This passage combines multiple purposes:

- **Informs** by providing scientific data and documenting observable changes
- **Persuades** by highlighting the human impact and implying an urgent need for action
- **Entertains** (secondarily) by using narrative techniques and human interest elements

The primary purpose appears to be informative, but the emotional human story and implications about necessary action reveal persuasive elements as well. This blending of purposes is common in long-form journalism and creative nonfiction.

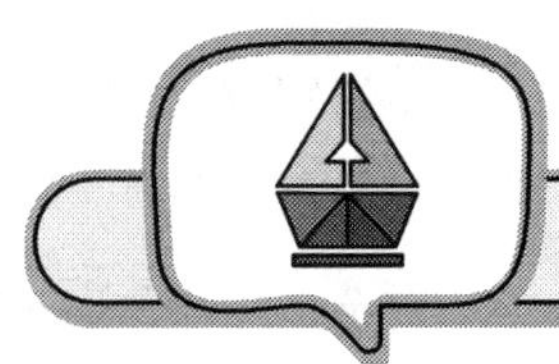

Week 5 • Practice Activity 1

Identifying Primary Purpose

Directions: Read each passage and determine whether its primary purpose is to inform, to persuade, or to entertain. Identify at least two specific pieces of evidence that support your answer.

Passage A: The process of photosynthesis converts light energy into chemical energy that plants use to grow. This transformation begins when pigments in the plant's chloroplasts, primarily chlorophyll, absorb sunlight. The captured light energy enables the plant to convert carbon dioxide and water into glucose (a sugar) and oxygen. The glucose provides energy for the plant's growth, while the oxygen is released into the atmosphere as a byproduct. This process is essential not only for plant survival but also for maintaining atmospheric oxygen levels that support animal life, making it one of the most important biochemical processes on Earth.

Purpose: ....

Evidence: ....

....

....

Passage B: We cannot afford to wait another decade to address climate change. While politicians debate theoretical targets for 2050, Pacific islands are disappearing, wildfires are destroying communities, and extreme weather events are becoming the norm rather than the exception. The latest IPCC report makes it clear: we have less than eight years to make substantial changes before reaching irreversible tipping points. The technology for transition already exists—what we lack is political will. Contact your representatives today and demand concrete action plans with immediate implementation timelines. Our children's future depends on the choices we make right now.

Purpose: ....

Evidence: ....

....

....

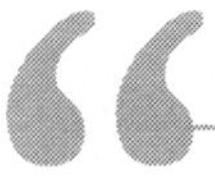

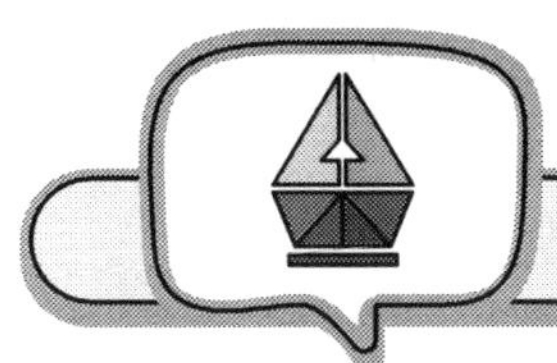

Key Concept #2: Explicit vs. Implicit Purpose

Why It Matters

Authors don't always directly state why they're writing. While some texts contain explicit purpose statements ("The aim of this essay is to examine..."), many communicate purpose implicitly through tone, structure, word choice, and other subtle elements. Developing the ability to recognize both explicit and implicit purpose helps you become a more sophisticated reader who can see beyond surface-level content to understand an author's true intentions.

Mastering this skill helps you:

- Identify an author's purpose even when it isn't directly stated.
- Recognize potential biases or hidden agendas in texts.
- Understand how various elements of a text contribute to its purpose.
- Analyze the relationship between stated and actual purposes in complex texts.

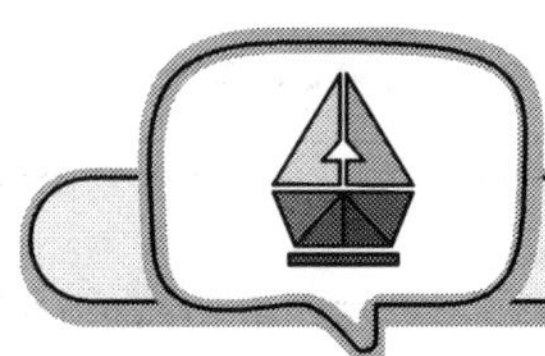

Week 5 • Reading for Author's Purpose

Recognizing Explicit and Implicit Purpose

Authors communicate their purpose both directly and indirectly. Learning to identify both explicit statements of purpose and implicit clues helps you determine why a text was written, even when the purpose isn't obvious.

Explicit Purpose is directly stated by the author, often in an introduction, thesis statement, or conclusion. Look for phrases like "This article explains...," "My goal is to persuade...," or "This essay analyzes..."

Implicit Purpose must be inferred from elements like tone, word choice, organization, and selection of details.

Here are key indicators that help you determine implicit purpose:

1. **Tone and word choice:** Emotional or charged language often signals persuasive intent, while neutral, technical language typically indicates informative purpose.

2. **Selection of details:** What information is included or omitted can reveal purpose. One-sided presentation suggests persuasion.

3. **Organizational patterns:** Problem-solution or cause-effect structures often indicate persuasive purpose, while chronological or classification patterns typically serve informative purposes.

4. **Use of rhetorical devices:** Frequent use of rhetorical questions, appeals to emotion, or call-to-action statements suggests persuasive intent.

5. **Visual elements:** In multimedia texts, dramatic images or empathic design elements may signal a persuasive purpose beyond what the words alone indicate.

Example 3: Identifying Explicit Purpose Statements

Explicit purpose statements directly tell readers why the author is writing. These statements often appear in introductions or conclusions and use clear language about the author's intentions.

Academic Article Introduction: "This study examines the impact of microplastic pollution on marine ecosystems in the South Pacific. By analyzing samples collected from twenty sites across five island nations, we aim to document current contamination levels and establish baseline data for future research. Additionally, we evaluate existing mitigation strategies and their effectiveness in reducing plastic waste in vulnerable coastal communities."

The explicit purpose statement identifies multiple goals:

- To examine microplastic pollution's impact (primary research purpose)
- To document current contamination levels (specific informative goal)
- To establish baseline data (future-oriented research purpose)
- To evaluate mitigation strategies (analytical/evaluative purpose)

This multifaceted purpose statement is typical of academic research, which often aims to not just present information but also analyze its significance and implications.

Speech Opening: "I stand before you today not merely to recount history, but to call each of us to action. My purpose is to convince you that the environmental challenges facing our nation are not insurmountable—but they do require our immediate and sustained commitment. By the time I conclude, I hope you will not only understand the scope of the problem but also feel empowered to become part of the solution."

This explicit purpose statement clearly identifies:

- A persuasive goal ("to call each of us to action," "to convince you")
- The specific attitude change desired (seeing problems as solvable but urgent)
- The intended outcome (audience feeling "empowered to become part of the solution")

The speaker leaves no doubt that the primary purpose is persuasion, not just information.

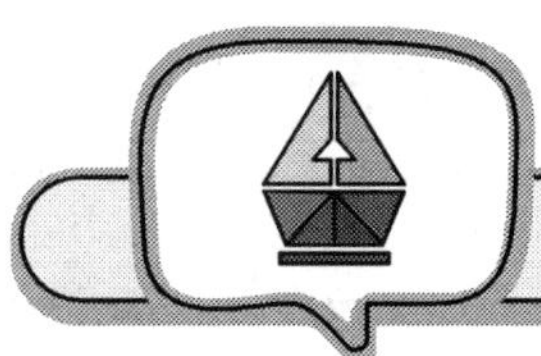

Example 4: Analyzing Implicit Purpose Through Textual Clues

Most texts don't contain explicit purpose statements, requiring readers to analyze various elements to determine the author's intentions.

Excerpt from a travel article: "The 'undiscovered paradise' of Costa Blanca is, in reality, a concrete jungle of high-rise hotels where tourists pack themselves onto crowded beaches like sardines in a tin. Local cuisine has been replaced by familiar fast-food chains, while souvenir shops selling mass-produced trinkets have pushed out traditional craftspeople. Those seeking an authentic Spanish experience would be wise to look elsewhere, perhaps to the less developed coastal towns further south, where tourism hasn't yet stripped away all traces of local culture."

Though this might appear to be an informative travel piece, several clues reveal an implicit persuasive purpose:

- **Negative tone and charged language:** "concrete jungle," "packed like sardines," "stripped away"
- **Contrast structure:** Setting up expectations ("undiscovered paradise") and then contradicting them
- **Direct recommendation:** Telling readers to "look elsewhere"
- **One-sided presentation:** Focusing only on negative aspects without balanced coverage
- **Value judgments:** Implying authentic experiences are superior to mainstream tourism

Without explicitly stating "I aim to persuade you to avoid Costa Blanca," the author clearly intends to influence readers' travel decisions through carefully selected details and evaluative language.

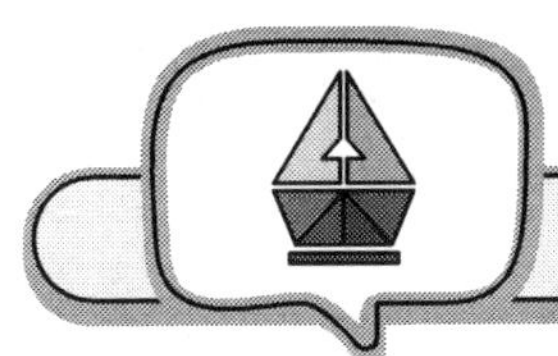

Week 5 • Practice Activity 2

Analyzing Explicit and Implicit Purpose

Directions: Read the following excerpt and then answer the questions that follow.

Excerpt from Gabriel García Márquez's Nobel Prize Acceptance Speech

Poets and beggars, musicians and prophets, warriors and scoundrels, all creatures of that unbridled reality, we have had to ask but little of imagination, for our crucial problem has been a lack of conventional means to render our lives believable. This, my friends, is the crux of our solitude.

For if these difficulties impede us, the European rational mind also works against us in the perception of our reality. It is only natural that they insist on measuring us with the same yardstick that they use to measure themselves, forgetting that the ravages of life are not the same for all, and that the quest for our own identity is just as arduous and bloody for us as it was for them. The interpretation of our reality through patterns not our own serves only to make us ever more unknown, ever less free, ever more solitary.

Faced with this awesome reality that through all of human time must have seemed a utopia, we, the inventors of tales, who will believe anything, feel entitled to believe that it is not yet too late to engage in the creation of a new and sweeping utopia of life, where no one will be able to decide for others how they die, where love will prove true and happiness be possible, and where the races condemned to one hundred years of solitude will have, at last and forever, a second opportunity on earth.

Question 1: What is García Márquez's explicit purpose in this excerpt?

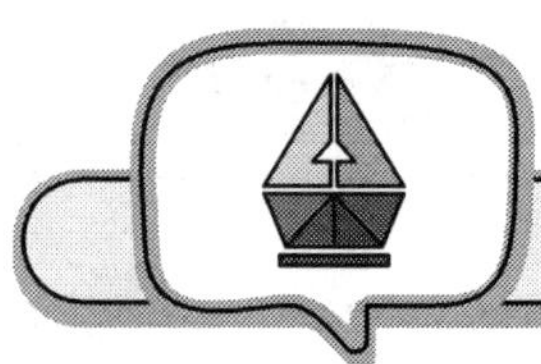

Week 5 • Practice Activity 2

Question 2: What implicit purposes can you identify in this passage?

Question 3: How does García Márquez combine informative, persuasive, and expressive elements in this excerpt? Give specific examples of each.

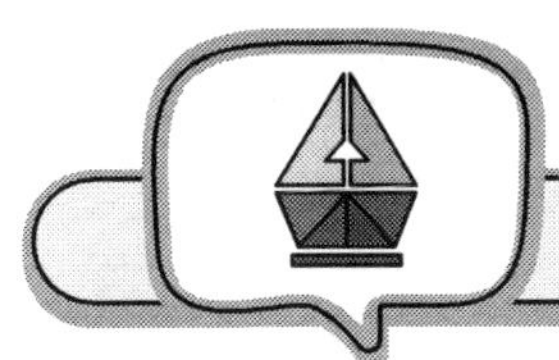

Week 5 • Practice Activity 3

Practice Activity #3: Analyzing Author's Purpose

Directions: Read the excerpt below and then answer the questions that follow.

Excerpt from "Nelson Mandela's Inaugural Address" (May, 1994)

Today, all of us do, by our presence here, and by our celebrations in other parts of our country and the world, confer glory and hope to newborn liberty. Out of the experience of an extraordinary human disaster that lasted too long, must be born a society of which all humanity will be proud of.

Our daily deeds as ordinary South Africans must produce an actual South African reality that will reinforce humanity's belief in justice, strengthen its confidence in the nobility of the human soul and sustain all our hopes for a glorious life for all.

The time for the healing of the wounds has come. The moment to bridge the chasms that divide us has come. The time to build is upon us. We have, at last, achieved our political emancipation. We pledge ourselves to liberate all our people from the continuing bondage of poverty, deprivation, suffering, gender and other discrimination.

We succeeded to take our last steps to freedom in conditions of relative peace. We commit ourselves to the construction of a complete, just and lasting peace. We have triumphed in the effort to implant hope in the breasts of the millions of our people. We enter into a covenant that we shall build the society in which all South Africans, both black and white, will be able to walk tall, without any fear in their hearts, assured of their inalienable right to human dignity—a rainbow nation at peace with itself and the world.

Question 1: What is Mandela's primary purpose in this excerpt from his inaugural address?

A. to announce new legislation that will define South Africa's democracy

B. to reflect on his personal political journey and struggles during apartheid

C. to critique the international community for failing to intervene in apartheid sooner

D. to unite the country by calling for healing, justice, and shared national purpose

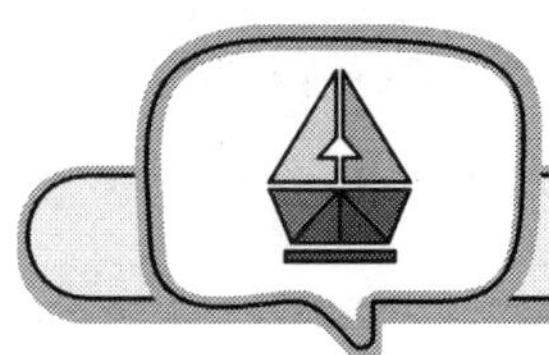

Week 5 • Practice Activity 3

Question 2: How does the historical context of South Africa's transition from apartheid to democracy shape the tone and message of Mandela's speech?

- **A.** It prompts a tone of vengeance and demands for retribution from the formerly oppressed.
- **B.** It encourages a focus on economic policies over emotional appeals.
- **C.** It informs a tone of reconciliation and a message of rebuilding a nation scarred by injustice.
- **D.** It requires Mandela to limit references to apartheid to avoid offending political opponents.

Question 3: Which of the following statements best reflects an explicit purpose expressed by Mandela in this speech?

- **A.** to call for unity and the building of a peaceful, just society
- **B.** to announce the official end of apartheid laws in South Africa
- **C.** to outline his detailed political strategy for economic recovery
- **D.** to warn former political opponents about future consequences

Question 4: Which of the following best conveys the implicit purpose behind Mandela's use of emotionally powerful language and repetition?

- **A.** to subtly critique the failures of colonial governments
- **B.** to persuade listeners that reconciliation is a moral and national imperative
- **C.** to present a neutral analysis of the new South African constitution
- **D.** to highlight his own political qualifications and experience

Wonderful work! Tomorrow, we'll explore how an author's purpose shapes the content and organization of texts.

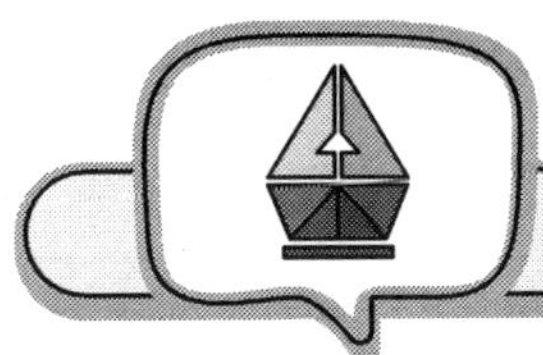

Analyzing How Purpose Shapes Content

By the end of this lesson, you'll be able to:

- Examine how an author's purpose influences their selection of evidence and details.
- Analyze how organizational patterns reflect different authorial intentions.
- Identify how tone, language choice, and stylistic elements support the purpose.
- Recognize how audience awareness affects an author's approach.

Key Concept #1: How Purpose Influences Content Selection

Why It Matters

An author's purpose doesn't just determine what they write—it shapes every choice they make about what information to include or exclude. Understanding this relationship helps you analyze why certain details appear in a text and what they reveal about the author's intentions. This awareness allows you to evaluate content more critically, recognizing what might be emphasized, downplayed, or omitted based on the author's goals.

Mastering this skill helps you:

- Identify potential gaps or biases in a text's coverage of a topic.
- Recognize how evidence is selected to support specific purposes.
- Evaluate the comprehensiveness and balance of information presented.
- Understand why different texts on the same topic may include very different content.

Content Selection and Author's Purpose

Authors make countless choices about what information to include and emphasize in their texts. These choices are directly guided by their purpose, whether they're trying to inform, persuade, entertain, or achieve some combination of these goals.

When analyzing how purpose influences content selection, consider these key aspects:

1. **Scope of information:** How broad or narrow is the coverage? Informative texts often provide comprehensive coverage, while persuasive texts may focus more narrowly on details that support their position.

2. Balance of perspectives: Are multiple viewpoints presented? Informative texts typically present balanced perspectives, while persuasive texts may emphasize one viewpoint.

3. Types of evidence: What kinds of support does the author provide? Scientific texts prioritize empirical data, persuasive texts may emphasize emotional examples, and narrative texts focus on character development and plot.

4. Depth of coverage: How detailed is the information? Technical texts for specialists include more depth than general-audience pieces on the same topic.

5. Inclusion/exclusion decisions: What information is notably absent? Sometimes what's left out reveals as much about purpose as what's included.

Example 1: Content Selection in Different Text Types

Let's examine how authors with different purposes cover the same topic—in this case, honeybees.

Scientific Article (Purpose: To Inform) "Worker honeybees (Apis mellifera) develop from fertilized eggs and comprise the majority of the colony population, numbering 20,000-80,000 individuals depending on seasonal conditions. These female bees progress through a series of age-related tasks: cleaning cells (days 1-2), nursing larvae (days 3-11), producing wax and building comb (days 12-17), guarding the hive entrance (days 18-21), and finally foraging for nectar and pollen (days 22+ until death). This temporal polyethism maximizes colony efficiency while allowing for task flexibility based on colony needs. Recent research indicates that epigenetic factors, rather than pure genetic determinism, may influence task transition timing."

Content choices reflecting an informative purpose:

- Precise terminology and scientific classification (Apis mellifera)
- Specific numerical data (population ranges, exact day ranges for tasks)
- Comprehensive coverage of worker bee development stages
- Neutral presentation of factual information
- Recent scientific developments included (epigenetic factors)
- Absence of value judgments or emotional appeal

Advocacy Article (Purpose: To Persuade) "Honeybees, the unsung heroes of our food system, are disappearing at an alarming rate. These tireless workers pollinate over 70% of the crops that provide 90% of the world's food, contributing an estimated $15 billion annually to the U.S. economy alone. Despite their crucial role, honeybee populations have plummeted by a devastating 30% annually in recent years due to the perfect storm of toxic pesticides, habitat loss, climate change, and disease. Without immediate action to ban neonicotinoid pesticides and restore native flowering habitats, we face a future of empty grocery shelves and skyrocketing food prices. The time to save our pollinators—and ourselves—is now."

Content choices reflecting persuasive purpose:

- Emotionally charged language ("unsung heroes," "alarming," "devastating")
- Statistics selected to emphasize importance and crisis (70% of crops, 90% of food)
- Economic impact highlighted ($15 billion) to demonstrate practical relevance
- Specific causes identified with emphasis on human-caused factors
- Clear solutions proposed with urgency
- Consequences of inaction explicitly stated to motivate response
- No mention of scientific debates or uncertainty about colony collapse causes

Children's Book (Purpose: To Entertain and Inform) "Buzzy the honeybee woke up excited for her first day as a forager. After weeks of taking care of baby bees and helping build the honeycomb, she was finally old enough to fly outside the hive to collect nectar! 'Remember to dance when you find flowers,' her friend Bella reminded her. 'That's how you'll show everyone else where to go!' Buzzy practiced her waggle dance one more time before flying out into the sunshine. She couldn't wait to explore the garden and bring back sweet nectar to make honey for her family."

Content choices reflecting entertainment with secondary informative purpose:

- Anthropomorphized bee character with emotions and personality
- Simplified explanation of bee roles and development
- Focus on the most visually appealing or interesting bee behaviors (waggle dance)
- Narrative structure with character dialogue
- Positive, upbeat language appropriate for young audience
- Selected factual elements (progression of bee tasks, communication through dancing)
- Omission of complex scientific details or concerning environmental issues

Each text covers honeybees but includes dramatically different information based on its purpose. The scientific article provides comprehensive, neutral information; the advocacy piece selects facts that emphasize crisis and human impact; and the children's book simplifies information while creating emotional engagement through story.

Example 2: Analyzing Inclusion and Omission Decisions

What authors choose to leave out can be just as revealing about their purpose as what they include. Consider these different accounts of a historical event:

History Textbook (Purpose: To Inform) "The 1960 independence of the Democratic Republic of Congo from Belgian colonial rule was followed by political instability and conflict. Prime Minister Patrice Lumumba, elected in May 1960, faced multiple challenges, including an army mutiny, the secession of mineral-rich Katanga Province, and tensions with former colonial authorities. In September 1960, Colonel Joseph Mobutu led a military coup that removed Lumumba from power. Lumumba was later arrested and, in January 1961, executed in circumstances that remain controversial. Documents declassified in the 2000s suggest involvement of both Belgian authorities and the United States CIA in his overthrow and death. Mobutu (later Mobutu Sese Seko) would rule the country for 32 years until 1997."

This informative account includes:

- Chronological presentation of key events
- Multiple factors contributing to instability
- Acknowledgment of controversial aspects
- Reference to later revelations about foreign involvement
- Long-term consequences (Mobutu's extended rule)

Anti-Colonial Essay (Purpose: To Persuade) "The assassination of Patrice Lumumba in 1961 represents one of the most shameful chapters in the West's violent suppression of African self-determination. Having won Congo's first democratic election, Lumumba committed the unforgivable sin in Cold War politics: asserting that Congo's vast mineral wealth should benefit its own people rather than Western corporations. Declassified documents have confirmed what many suspected: the CIA and Belgian operatives orchestrated his removal and brutal murder, replacing him with the compliant dictator Mobutu who would protect Western mining interests for decades while brutally oppressing his people. The blood of Congo's subsequent civil wars, which have claimed over five million lives, stains the hands of those colonial powers who could not tolerate genuine African independence."

This persuasive account:

- Focuses heavily on Western involvement rather than internal factors
- Emphasizes economic motivations (mineral wealth, corporate interests)
- Uses emotionally charged language ("shameful," "brutal," "blood stains")
- Draws direct causal connections between the assassination and later conflicts
- Provides specific victim counts to highlight the human toll
- Omits details about the army mutiny or Katanga secession that might complicate the narrative

The persuasive essay's omissions and emphasis clearly serve its anti-colonial viewpoint, while the textbook attempts more balanced coverage. Neither account is necessarily "wrong," but each selects and emphasizes information that aligns with its purpose.

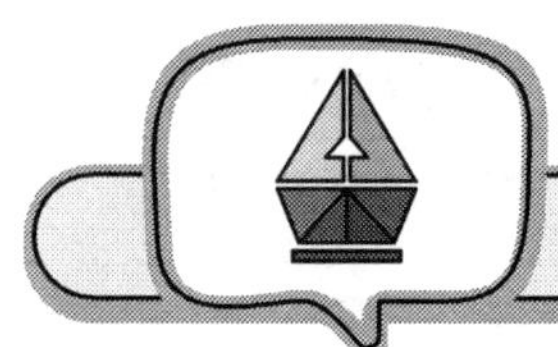

Week 5 • Practice Activity 1

Analyzing Content Selection

Directions: Read the two passages below about the same historical event. Identify the author's purpose for each passage and explain how content selection reflects that purpose.

Passage A: On August 28, 1963, approximately 250,000 people participated in the March on Washington for Jobs and Freedom. The demonstration was organized by a coalition of civil rights, labor, and religious organizations, including the NAACP, SCLC, and UAW. Participants gathered at the Washington Monument and marched to the Lincoln Memorial, where the day's program included speeches from John Lewis, Roy Wilkins, and Whitney Young, among others. The event is perhaps best remembered for Martin Luther King Jr.'s "I Have a Dream" speech. The March occurred during a pivotal period in the civil rights movement, following Birmingham demonstrations earlier that year and preceding the Civil Rights Act of 1964. Initially, President Kennedy had discouraged the March, fearing potential violence, but later endorsed it after organizers agreed to certain conditions, including ending the demonstration before dark.

Author's purpose: ....

Explanation: ....

....

Passage B: The 1963 March on Washington represented a pivotal moment in America's journey toward fulfilling its founding promise of equality. Against the backdrop of fire hoses and police dogs in Birmingham, lunch counter sit-ins across the South, and the assassination of Medgar Evers, 250,000 Americans—Black and white, young and old, from every corner of the nation—converged on the National Mall to demand justice. Their collective presence transformed abstract political issues into moral imperatives that could no longer be ignored. When Martin Luther King Jr. stood before the Lincoln Memorial and shared his dream of a nation where character, not color, determined one's destiny, he gave voice to America's highest aspirations. The March demonstrated the power of nonviolent protest and moral witness, creating unstoppable momentum for the landmark civil rights legislation that would follow. Its legacy reminds us that ordinary citizens, standing together in peaceful solidarity, can bend the arc of history toward justice.

Author's purpose: ....

Explanation: ....

....

Key Concept #2: Organizational Patterns and Purpose

Why It Matters

How authors structure their writing reveals a great deal about their purpose. Different organizational patterns naturally support different goals—chronological order helps tell stories, problem-solution structures build persuasive arguments, and classification systems organize informative content. By recognizing these patterns, you can better understand how an author is trying to guide your thinking and what response they hope to elicit.

Mastering this skill helps you:

- Identify an author's purpose by analyzing their organizational choices.
- Predict how information will develop based on recognized patterns.
- Understand how structure contributes to the effectiveness of different text types.
- Recognize when organizational patterns are being used to influence your perspective.

Common Organizational Patterns and Their Purposes

The way authors organize information directly supports their purpose. Here are common organizational patterns and how they connect to specific authorial goals:

1. **Chronological Organization** arranges information by time sequence.
   - ◇ Common in: Narratives, histories, process explanations
   - ◇ Supports: Informing about sequences, entertaining through storytelling
2. **Cause-Effect Organization** shows relationships between events and their results.
   - ◇ Common in: Scientific explanations, policy arguments
   - ◇ Supports: Informing about relationships, persuading by showing consequences
3. **Problem-Solution Organization** identifies an issue and proposes resolutions.
   - ◇ Common in: Persuasive essays, business proposals
   - ◇ Supports: Persuading readers to accept a proposed solution

4. **Compare-Contrast Organization** examines similarities and differences.
    - ◇ Common in: Product reviews, literary analysis
    - ◇ Supports: Informing about relationships, persuading through evaluation
5. **Classification/Categorization** groups related items or concepts.
    - ◇ Common in: Scientific texts, instructional materials
    - ◇ Supports: Organizing complex information for clearer understanding
6. **Spatial Organization** arranges details by physical location or relationship.
    - ◇ Common in: Descriptive writing, travel literature
    - ◇ Supports: Creating vivid mental images, often for entertainment or engagement
7. **Order of Importance** presents ideas from most to least important (or reverse).
    - ◇ Common in: News articles, argumentative essays
    - ◇ Supports: Emphasizing key points for persuasive impact or informational priority

Example 3: Analyzing Organization in Scientific Writing

Scientific articles often use organizational patterns that support their informative purpose. Let's examine how a scientific article about climate change in the Pacific Islands uses organization to achieve its goals:

Scientific Article Structure:

- **Introduction:** "This study examines climate change impacts on Pacific Island nations, with particular focus on sea level rise effects in Tuvalu, Kiribati, and the Marshall Islands. Drawing on ten years of observational data and community-based research, we document current conditions and project future scenarios based on multiple climate models."
- **Methods:** "We collected tidal gauge measurements from fifteen locations across the three island groups between 2010-2020. Satellite altimetry data supplemented ground-based observations. Additionally, we conducted interviews with 120 community members regarding observed environmental changes and adaptation strategies..."

- **Results:** "Sea levels across all study sites showed an average rise of 7.8mm annually over the study period, exceeding the global average of 3.6mm. Figure 1 illustrates the variation between individual monitoring stations. Salt water intrusion affected 42% of measured agricultural plots, with Kiribati experiencing the most severe impacts (Table 3)..."
- **Discussion:** "These findings indicate accelerating sea level rise compared to previous decades' measurements. The data support projections that large portions of the studied islands may become uninhabitable within 25-50 years without significant adaptation measures or global emissions reductions. Our results contradict assertions that Pacific Island nations are experiencing normal cyclical sea level variations..."
- **Conclusion:** "This research provides empirical documentation of climate change impacts already affecting Pacific Island communities. Future research should focus on effective adaptation strategies that incorporate both modern technology and traditional knowledge systems."

This organization reflects an informative purpose through:

- **Standard scientific structure** (IMRD format) that prioritizes methodological transparency
- **Logical progression** from what was studied, to how it was studied, to what was found, to what it means
- **Clear separation** of objective findings from interpretive discussion
- **Neutral presentation** of methods and results before offering interpretations
- **Comprehensive documentation** of procedures to allow for verification or replication
- **Visual data presentation** referenced to supplement written explanation

This organizational pattern emphasizes systematic knowledge-building rather than emotional appeal or narrative engagement, perfectly supporting its informative purpose.

Example 4: Analyzing Organization in Persuasive Writing

Persuasive texts often use organizational patterns specifically designed to build compelling arguments. Let's examine how a persuasive speech on climate change might be structured:

Climate Action Speech Structure:

- **Attention-grabbing opening:** "As I stand before you today, the village where my grandmother was born no longer exists. It now lies beneath the waves of the Pacific Ocean, another casualty in our planet's climate emergency."
- **Problem statement:** "Pacific Island nations contribute less than 0.03% of global carbon emissions, yet they face disproportionate consequences of climate change. Sea level rise has already forced communities to relocate, salt water intrusion has devastated crops, and increasingly severe cyclones threaten infrastructure that cannot be easily rebuilt."
- **Causes and responsibility:** "This crisis stems directly from carbon emissions produced primarily by industrialized nations. The average American produces 15.5 metric tons of CO_2 annually, while the average Pacific Islander produces less than 1 ton. This stark disparity raises profound questions of climate justice and responsibility."
- **Solution proposal:** "We must take three immediate actions. First, developed nations must meet and exceed their Paris Agreement commitments to reduce emissions. Second, climate finance must be directed to frontline communities for adaptation and mitigation. Third, immigration policies must be reformed to acknowledge and accommodate climate refugees."
- **Call to action:** "Today, I ask you not just for sympathy but for solidarity. Contact your representatives to demand climate legislation, divest from fossil fuel companies, and support organizations working directly with affected communities. The time for debate has passed—the time for action is now, before more islands disappear forever."

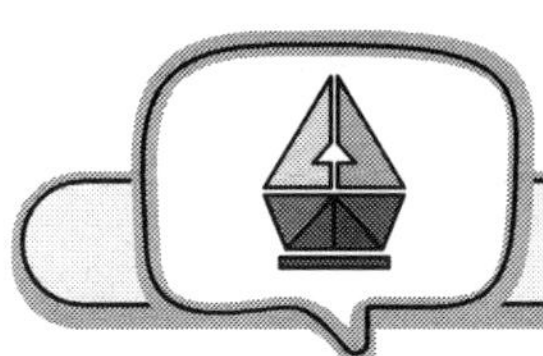

This organization reflects a persuasive purpose through:

- **Emotional opening** to create immediate engagement and urgency
- **Problem-solution structure** that identifies issues before presenting solutions
- **Cause-effect relationships** that establish responsibility
- **Rule of three** in the solution section for memorability and impact
- **Specific call to action** that gives the audience clear next steps
- **Circular structure** that returns to the opening image for emotional reinforcement

Unlike the scientific article, this organization prioritizes building emotional connection and motivating specific actions rather than simply informing. The speech moves strategically from personal story to global problem to individual responsibility, guiding listeners toward the desired response.

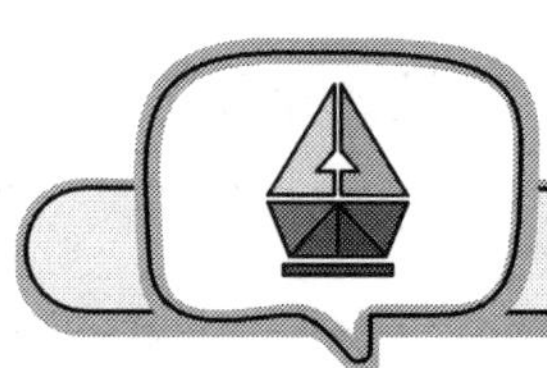

Week 5 • Practice Activity 2

Organizational Analysis

Directions: Read the excerpt and then answer the questions that follow.

Excerpt from "Climate Change Impacts on Pacific Island Nations"

1. Introduction: Climate change presents existential challenges to Pacific Island nations, with rising sea levels, increasing ocean acidification, and intensifying storm patterns threatening both physical territories and cultural continuity. This paper synthesizes current research on climate impacts specific to Pacific Island contexts while highlighting innovative adaptation strategies emerging from affected communities.

2. Methodology: This study employs mixed methods, combining quantitative analysis of climate data from 18 monitoring stations across the Pacific region with qualitative research conducted in partnership with indigenous communities in Tuvalu, Kiribati, and the Marshall Islands. Participatory action research frameworks guided community engagement, ensuring research questions and adaptation priorities reflected local concerns rather than external assumptions.

3. Results:

3.1 Sea Level Rise Measurements: Tidal gauge data indicate sea level rise averaging 7.6mm annually across study sites during 2010-2020, exceeding global means by approximately 300%. Figure 1 illustrates geographical variation, with northern Marshall Islands experiencing the most pronounced increases (9.2mm annually).

3.2 Community Impact Assessment: Interview and focus group data reveal significant consequences of observed environmental changes. Table 2 summarizes reported impacts on food security, with 87% of participants describing reduced agricultural productivity due to saltwater intrusion. Cultural impacts emerged as equally significant, with 73% reporting disruption to traditional practices tied to specific locations now threatened by inundation.

4. Discussion: Our findings challenge several prevalent narratives in climate adaptation literature. First, data contradict the portrayal of Pacific Islanders as passive victims awaiting external assistance, instead documenting proactive, culturally-grounded responses. Second, results highlight the inadequacy of technological solutions that fail to account for cultural and spiritual connections to place. Finally, the research demonstrates the necessity of centering indigenous knowledge in climate adaptation frameworks.

5. Conclusion: As global temperatures continue to rise, Pacific Island nations face intensifying challenges that demand urgent international action on emissions reduction. Simultaneously, the adaptive strategies documented in this study demonstrate the critical importance of supporting locally-developed, culturally-appropriate responses that honor the agency and knowledge of affected communities. Future research should focus on mechanisms for integrating traditional ecological knowledge into climate policy while ensuring just distribution of adaptation resources.

Question 1: What is the primary purpose of this scientific article?

A. to persuade international governments to increase funding for Pacific Island tourism

B. to report evidence of sea level rise and describe how Pacific Island communities are responding with culturally grounded adaptation strategies

C. to critique meteorological agencies for underestimating storm risks in the Pacific region

D. to propose the relocation of all Pacific Islanders to higher-elevation territories

Question 2: How do the "Community Impact Assessment" and "Local Adaptation Strategies" sections reflect a secondary purpose of the article?

A. They promote economic growth strategies based on climate data.

B. They emphasize the role of external aid organizations in shaping policy.

C. They challenge the stereotype of Pacific Islanders as passive and instead highlight agency and resilience.

D. They provide instructions for replicating scientific experiments in other regions.

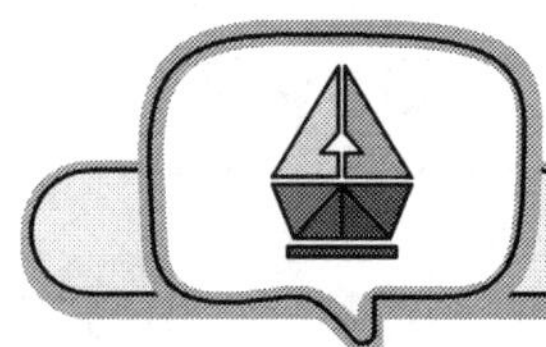

Key Concept #3: Audience Awareness and Purpose

Why It Matters

Authors always write with a specific audience in mind, and their understanding of that audience fundamentally shapes their content, organization, and style. Recognizing how authors adapt their approach for different readers helps you analyze why they make particular choices and how effectively they connect with their intended audience. This awareness also helps you become more discerning about whether you are part of the primary audience for a text.

Mastering this skill helps you:

- Identify the intended audience for different texts.
- Recognize how authors adjust their approach for specific readers.
- Evaluate whether a text is appropriately designed for its audience.
- Understand when you may not be the primary audience for a text.

How Audience Awareness Shapes Writing

Skilled authors carefully tailor their writing to meet the needs, interests, and background knowledge of their intended audience. This audience awareness influences nearly every aspect of a text:

1. **Vocabulary and terminology:** Technical terms for specialists versus simplified explanations for general readers
2. **Background information:** Extensive context for novices versus minimal review for experts
3. **Tone and formality:** Scholarly language for academic readers versus conversational style for popular audiences
4. **Examples and references:** Culturally specific illustrations that resonate with the target audience
5. **Complexity and depth:** Detailed coverage for advanced readers versus accessible overviews for beginners
6. **Persuasive appeals:** Logical arguments for analytical audiences versus emotional stories for general readers
7. **Visual elements:** Technical diagrams for specialists versus engaging illustrations for broader audiences

Example 5: Adapting Content for Different Audiences

The same information can be presented very differently depending on the intended audience. Consider these three passages explaining the same concept—coral bleaching—for different readers:

For Middle School Students: "Corals might look like rocks, but they're actually tiny animals that live together in colonies. These coral animals have special plant-like organisms called zooxanthellae living inside them—think of them as roommates that help each other out! The zooxanthellae provide food to the coral through photosynthesis (using sunlight to make energy) and give corals their beautiful colors. But when ocean water gets too hot due to climate change, the coral gets stressed and kicks out its colorful roommates. Without the zooxanthellae, the coral turns white—that's coral bleaching. Bleached corals aren't dead yet, but they're starving without their food-producing partners and will die if the water doesn't cool down soon enough for the zooxanthellae to move back in."

For General Adult Readers: "Coral bleaching, a phenomenon increasingly observed in reefs worldwide, occurs when corals expel the algae that live within their tissues. These algae, called zooxanthellae, normally provide corals with food through photosynthesis and give them their distinctive colors. When ocean temperatures rise even 1-2°C above normal seasonal maximums for extended periods, the relationship between coral and algae breaks down. The stressed coral expels the zooxanthellae, revealing the white calcium carbonate skeleton beneath—hence the term "bleaching." While bleached corals aren't immediately dead, they've lost their primary food source and become vulnerable. Without conditions improving to allow the zooxanthellae to return, mass coral mortality often follows, devastating entire reef ecosystems."

For Marine Biology Researchers: "Thermal stress-induced coral bleaching events have increased in frequency and severity over the past three decades, corresponding with rising sea surface temperatures (SSTs). The breakdown of the coral-dinoflagellate symbiosis occurs when prolonged thermal anomalies of >1°C above maximum monthly means trigger the overproduction of reactive oxygen species in Symbiodiniaceae photosystems. This oxidative stress leads to cellular damage and subsequent expulsion of the endosymbiotic algae, resulting in the visible paling of coral tissues as the calcium carbonate skeleton becomes visible.

While some coral species demonstrate higher thermal tolerance thresholds or recovery capacity, meta-analysis indicates that post-bleaching recovery is significantly compromised when bleaching events occur in consecutive years, as documented in the 2016-2017 mass bleaching on the Great Barrier Reef. Recent transcriptomic studies suggest that epigenetic modifications may influence bleaching susceptibility, potentially offering pathways for adaptive responses under predicted climate scenarios."

Each version contains the core concept of coral bleaching, but differs dramatically in:

- **Vocabulary:** Simple metaphors for students ("roommates") versus technical terminology for researchers ("endosymbiotic algae," "oxidative stress")
- **Detail level:** Basic mechanism for students versus cellular processes and species-specific responses for researchers
- **Background knowledge assumed:** Middle school passage explains photosynthesis; researcher passage assumes understanding of complex biological concepts
- **Supporting information:** Student passage omits specific temperature thresholds and statistical trends included for researchers
- **Tone:** Conversational and reassuring for younger readers versus formal and technical for an academic audience

These adaptations reflect the authors' awareness of what different audiences need to understand the concept effectively.

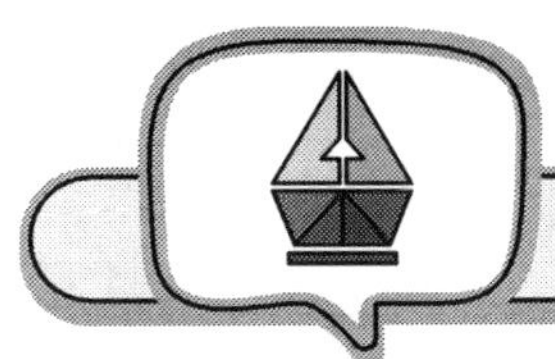

Example 6: Audience-Specific Persuasive Appeals

When persuading different audiences, authors select different types of evidence and appeals based on what will resonate most effectively with specific readers.

Consider how an article advocating for climate change action might approach different audiences:

For Business Leaders: "Climate action represents not merely an environmental imperative but a significant economic opportunity. Companies implementing sustainable practices have demonstrated 27% higher profit margins compared to industry peers, according to McKinsey's 2023 global survey. First-movers in renewable energy technology are capturing emerging markets worth an estimated $2.15 trillion annually by 2030. Additionally, businesses with strong environmental policies report 41% better employee retention rates, reducing costly turnover. With investors increasingly prioritizing ESG metrics and customers demonstrating a willingness to pay premium prices for sustainable products, the competitive advantage of climate leadership is clear. Those who adapt proactively will thrive in the low-carbon economy; those who delay risk obsolescence."

For Religious Community Members: "Our sacred texts call us to be faithful stewards of Creation, caring for this divine gift with wisdom and compassion. When we witness the suffering of communities devastated by intensifying storms, extended droughts, and rising seas, we are reminded of our moral responsibility to protect the vulnerable. Pope Francis reminds us in Laudato Si that "the climate is a common good, belonging to all and meant for all." Similarly, the Islamic Declaration on Global Climate Change states that we have a religious duty to "care for the gifts He has given us, including the natural world." By embracing clean energy, sustainable practices, and simpler lifestyles, we honor these spiritual teachings while creating a more just world where all of God's children can thrive."

For Parents: "The decisions we make today will determine what kind of world our children inherit tomorrow. Already, pediatricians report increasing cases of asthma and respiratory illness linked to climate-influenced air quality. Schools in the Southwest regularly cancel outdoor activities due to extreme heat, while those in coastal regions develop evacuation plans for intensifying hurricanes. Children born today will experience seven times more heatwaves and three times more river floods than their grandparents, according to research published in Science.

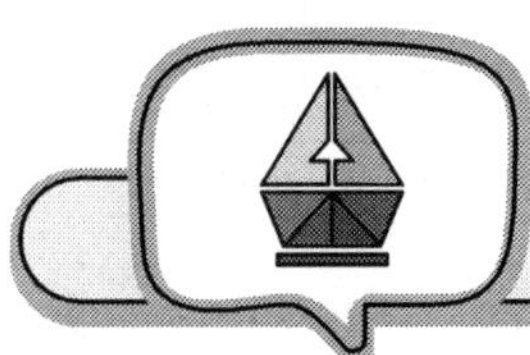

As parents, we have always made sacrifices to secure our children's future, from late nights helping with homework to saving for college. Climate action represents another crucial investment in their wellbeing, ensuring they inherit a world of opportunity rather than crisis."

Each appeal targets specific values and priorities:

- **Business audience:** Economic data, profit potential, competitive advantage
- **Religious audience:** Moral responsibility, spiritual teachings, ethical frameworks
- **Parent audience:** Children's health and safety, future impacts, emotional connection

The core message—climate action is necessary—remains consistent, but the supporting evidence and framing shift dramatically based on what will motivate each specific audience most effectively.

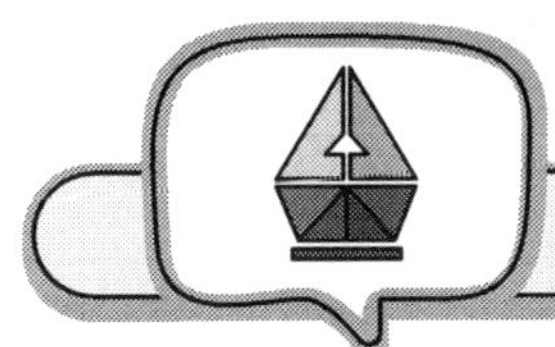

Week 5 • Practice Activity 3

Analyzing Audience Awareness and Purpose

Directions: Read the passage below and answer the questions that follow.

From a brochure promoting a local historical museum: Step into the past and bring your family along for a journey through time! The Eastwood Historical Museum isn't just a place for quiet reflection—it's a hands-on adventure for all ages. Dress up like 19th-century pioneers, churn real butter in our living history kitchen, and explore the stories of Eastwood's earliest residents. With rotating exhibits, scavenger hunts for kids, and weekend craft workshops, we make learning local history fun. Whether you're a lifelong resident or a first-time visitor, come discover why history still matters today!

Question 1: Who is the most likely intended audience for this passage?

A. academic historians researching local migration patterns

B. city council members deciding on museum funding

C. families looking for an educational and fun weekend activity

D. high school students studying for a history exam

Question 2: Which element of the passage most clearly reflects the author's awareness of the audience?

A. the mention of 19th-century migration routes

B. the inclusion of weekend craft workshops and kid-friendly activities

C. the reference to Eastwood's founding date

D. the formal tone and technical language used

Question 3: What is the primary purpose of this passage?

A. to persuade families to visit the museum by making history feel exciting and interactive

B. to critique the lack of historical education in public schools

C. to inform readers about the economic impact of tourism in Eastwood

D. to explain the historical significance of Eastwood's founding events

Excellent! Tomorrow, we'll focus on evaluating the effectiveness of an author's approach.

Evaluating Effectiveness of Author's Approach

By the end of this lesson, you'll be able to:

- Assess how successfully an author achieves their intended purpose.
- Evaluate the appropriateness of rhetorical choices for specific audiences.
- Analyze how cultural context affects the effectiveness of various approaches.
- Identify factors that enhance or diminish a text's impact and persuasiveness.

Key Concept #1: Criteria for Evaluating Effectiveness

Why It Matters

Not all texts succeed equally well at achieving their purposes. Learning to evaluate a text's effectiveness helps you become a more discerning reader who can recognize what makes communication powerful and persuasive. This critical awareness enables you to assess the quality of information you encounter and to improve your own writing by applying successful techniques.

Mastering this skill helps you:

- Distinguish between effective and ineffective communication.
- Identify specific elements that contribute to a text's success or failure.
- Apply successful techniques to your own writing and speaking.
- Make informed judgments about the value and quality of texts you encounter.

Criteria for Evaluating Different Text Types

Different types of writing require different evaluation criteria based on their purpose. Understanding these specific standards helps you assess texts more accurately.

For Informative Texts, effectiveness depends on:

1. **Accuracy:** Is the information factually correct and current?
2. **Clarity:** Is complex information presented in an understandable way?
3. **Comprehensiveness:** Does the text cover the topic thoroughly?

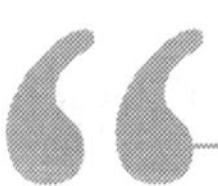

4. **Organization:** Is the information structured logically for easy comprehension?
5. **Objectivity:** Does the text present balanced information without bias?
6. **Relevance:** Does the content focus on what matters most to the audience?
7. **Credibility:** Are claims supported by reliable evidence and expertise?

For Persuasive Texts, effectiveness depends on:

1. **Logical reasoning:** Are arguments clearly reasoned and supported?
2. **Credible evidence:** Does the text provide trustworthy support for claims?
3. **Addressing counterarguments:** Does it acknowledge and respond to opposing views?
4. **Appropriate appeals:** Does it effectively use logical, emotional, and ethical appeals?
5. **Audience awareness:** Does it connect with the specific audience's values and concerns?
6. **Call to action:** Does it clearly indicate what readers should think or do?
7. **Ethical approach:** Does it persuade without manipulation or deception?

For Narrative/Expressive Texts, effectiveness depends on:

1. **Engagement:** Does it capture and maintain reader interest?
2. **Authenticity:** Does it create believable characters, situations, or emotions?
3. **Imagery and description:** Does it create vivid mental pictures?
4. **Coherence:** Does the narrative flow logically and meaningfully?
5. **Emotional impact:** Does it evoke intended emotional responses?
6. **Thematic depth:** Does it communicate meaningful themes or insights?
7. **Originality:** Does it offer fresh perspectives or approaches?

Example 1: Evaluating an Informative Text

Let's evaluate this excerpt from an informative article about climate change using the relevant criteria:

Excerpt from a climate change article: "Rising global temperatures are causing significant changes to Pacific Island nations. Sea levels in this region have risen approximately 3mm per year since 1993, according to satellite data analyzed by the Pacific Climate Change Science Program. This rate slightly exceeds the global average. Higher water levels contribute to coastal erosion, saltwater intrusion into freshwater sources, and increased flooding during storm events. For low-lying atoll nations like Kiribati, where the average elevation is just two meters above sea level, these changes pose existential challenges."

Effectiveness evaluation:

- **Accuracy:** The article provides specific, verifiable data (3mm annual rise, dates, average elevation) rather than vague generalizations.
- **Clarity:** Complex climate concepts are explained in straightforward language. Terms like "saltwater intrusion" are immediately clarified by their effects.
- **Organization:** Information flows logically from global phenomenon → regional impact → specific example, creating a clear causal sequence.
- **Objectivity:** The language remains factual without overtly emotional terms, though "existential challenges" acknowledges severity while remaining accurate.
- **Credibility:** The article cites a specific scientific program as its data source, enhancing reliability.

Example 2: Evaluating a Persuasive Text

Now let's evaluate the effectiveness of a persuasive speech excerpt using relevant criteria:

Excerpt from a speech about climate action: "The science is clear, but our resolve must be clearer. While Pacific Islands contribute less than 0.03% of global carbon emissions, they face the most immediate consequences of climate inaction. Is this the justice we stand for in the 21st century?

Some argue that addressing climate change is too expensive. But consider this: the World Bank estimates that without action, climate impacts will reduce global GDP by up to 18% by 2050. Meanwhile, transitioning to clean energy creates three times more jobs per dollar invested than fossil fuels.

Today, I ask you to support legislation requiring 50% emissions reduction by 2030. Call your representatives. Divest from fossil fuel companies. Join community climate initiatives. The time for debate has passed—the time for action is now."

Effectiveness evaluation:

- **Logical reasoning:** The speech uses causal reasoning (inaction → consequences) and cost-benefit analysis (economic costs vs. benefits).
- **Credible evidence:** The speech cites specific statistics and sources (World Bank estimates, job creation figures).
- **Addressing counterarguments:** The speech acknowledges opposing economic concerns and directly counters them.
- **Appropriate appeals:** The speech balances logical appeals (statistics), emotional appeals (questions about justice), and ethical appeals (fairness).
- **Call to action:** The speech provides multiple specific actions rather than vague encouragement.

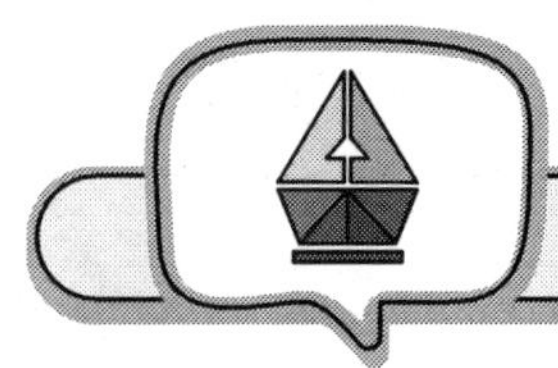

Evaluating Effectiveness

Directions: Read the excerpts below and identify its purpose. Then evaluate how effectively each achieves its purpose by identifying specific strengths and weaknesses.

Excerpt A: From a scientific article on coral reef conservation

The deterioration of coral reef ecosystems represents a significant ecological concern, with approximately 50% of global reef systems exhibiting substantial decline over the past three decades. Multiple anthropogenic stressors contribute to this degradation, including ocean acidification (pH reduction of 0.1 units since pre-industrial era), sea temperature anomalies exceeding local thermal thresholds, sedimentation from coastal development, and direct physical damage from extractive activities. Recent research indicates that reef resilience varies significantly based on local conditions, with some regions demonstrating enhanced recovery capacity despite global pressures. Conservation interventions focusing on reducible local stressors have demonstrated efficacy in preserving reef function even amid climate-driven challenges.

Purpose: ....

Strengths: ....

Weaknesses: ....

Excerpt B: From a travel blog post about visiting coral reefs

The moment I dipped below the surface, I entered another world. The water was so clear it felt like flying rather than swimming as I hovered above a metropolis of coral in every shape and color imaginable—delicate purple fans waving in the current, massive brain corals with their hypnotic patterns, and branching staghorns reaching toward the sunlight. Tiny electric-blue fish darted in and out of crevices while a curious parrotfish, its scales shimmering like a rainbow, examined me before returning to its constant munching on coral. It broke my heart to think these underwater wonderlands might disappear in my lifetime. Later, our guide showed us a bleached section of reef—a ghostly white cemetery that once pulsed with the same vibrant life we'd just witnessed. I surfaced from that dive a changed person, understanding for the first time what we stand to lose.

Purpose: ....

Strengths: ....

Weaknesses: ....

Key Concept #2: Audience Response and Effectiveness

Why It Matters

A text's effectiveness ultimately depends on how well it connects with its intended audience. What works for one group of readers may fail completely with another. Learning to analyze how audience characteristics influence reception helps you understand why certain approaches succeed or fail and how authors can better tailor their communication to specific readers.

Mastering this skill helps you:

- Predict how different audiences might respond to the same content.
- Identify mismatches between an authorial approach and audience needs.
- Adapt your own communication for specific audiences.
- Understand when texts might be ineffective due to audience factors rather than content.

Analyzing Audience-Text Relationship

A text's effectiveness depends greatly on how well it aligns with its audience's characteristics, including:

1. **Background knowledge:** Does the text assume appropriate prior knowledge?
2. **Values and beliefs:** Does the content connect with what the audience cares about?
3. **Reading level and vocabulary:** Is the language accessible but not condescending?
4. **Cultural context:** Does the approach respect cultural norms and references?
5. **Interests and motivation:** Does the text engage the audience on topics they find relevant?
6. **Expectations and preferences:** Does the form and style match what the audience expects?
7. **Resistance factors:** Does the approach address potential skepticism or opposition?

Example 3: Analyzing Audience-Text Alignment

Let's analyze how the same message might be received by different audiences based on how it's presented:

Message: "Reducing meat consumption has environmental benefits."

Version A (Academic Journal Article): "A meta-analysis of 153 studies indicates that animal agriculture contributes significantly to greenhouse gas emissions, with beef production generating an average of 99.48 kg CO_2-equivalent per kg protein compared to 20.41 kg CO_2-eq for poultry and 7.47 kg CO_2-eq for legumes. Transitioning from high-beef to plant-forward diets could reduce individual dietary carbon footprints by 30-50%."

Audience alignment analysis:

- **Effective for:** Academic researchers, environmental scientists, policy analysts
- **Ineffective for:** General public, younger readers, non-specialists

This version works for academic audiences because of its precise data, technical terminology, and objective tone. It would likely fail with general audiences due to overwhelming detail without practical guidance.

Version B (Popular Magazine Article): "What if you could fight climate change with your fork? The beef burger on your plate comes with a hefty environmental price tag, producing about 20 times more greenhouse gases than a veggie burger. Think of it this way: swapping just one beef-based meal for a plant-based one each day is like taking your car off the road for 320 miles every month! The good news? You don't have to go vegetarian overnight. Even small changes make a difference."

Audience alignment analysis:

- **Effective for:** General readers, environmentally concerned citizens
- **Ineffective for:** Academic specialists, highly knowledgeable environmentalists

This version works for general audiences through its conversational tone, relatable comparisons, acknowledgment of potential resistance, and practical steps. Specialists might find it too simplified without a methodological context.

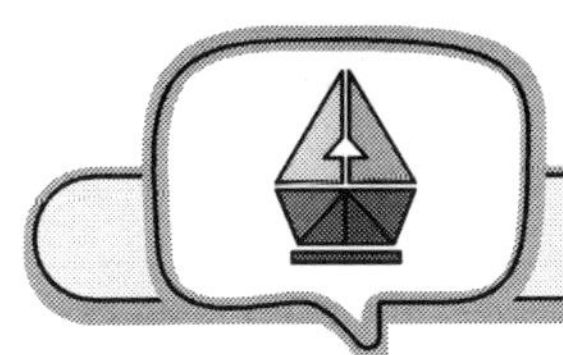

Audience Analysis

Directions: For each passage below, identify the likely intended audience and explain how specific elements of the text are tailored to that audience.

Passage A: Studies indicate that adolescents require approximately 8-10 hours of sleep per night for optimal cognitive functioning and emotional regulation. However, biological changes during puberty often shift circadian rhythms toward later sleep onset and awakening times, creating a mismatch with typical school start times. This discrepancy between biological needs and institutional schedules contributes to chronic sleep deprivation among teenagers, with potential consequences including impaired academic performance, increased risk-taking behavior, and elevated rates of depression and anxiety. Educational institutions implementing later start times (e.g., 8:30 AM or later) have documented improvements in attendance, decreased tardiness, reduced disciplinary incidents, and enhanced academic outcomes.

Intended Audience: ....

Explanation: ....

....

....

Passage B: Hey there! So you're thinking about going vegetarian but don't know where to start? No worries—I was totally in your shoes last year! The biggest game-changer for me was NOT trying to go cold turkey (pun intended 😂). Instead, I started with just two meatless days a week. This gave me time to experiment with new recipes without feeling overwhelmed. My absolute FAVORITE discovery was buffalo cauliflower "wings" (recipe link in bio!) that satisfied my junk food cravings. Another tip: don't just remove meat from your plate—replace it with something filling like beans, lentils, or tofu. Otherwise, you'll be reaching for snacks an hour later! Don't stress about being "perfect" either. This isn't an all-or-nothing deal! Every plant-based meal makes a difference for your health and the planet. Drop a comment if you have questions or need recipe ideas! #VeggieNewbies

Intended Audience: ....

Explanation: ....

....

....

Key Concept #3: Evaluating Rhetorical Strategies

Why It Matters

Authors use various rhetorical strategies—techniques designed to enhance the impact and persuasiveness of their writing. Learning to recognize and evaluate these strategies helps you understand how writers influence readers' thinking and emotional responses. This awareness allows you to assess whether these techniques are being used ethically and effectively.

Mastering this skill helps you:

- Identify specific techniques authors use to influence readers.
- Evaluate whether rhetorical choices enhance or undermine a text's purpose.
- Distinguish between effective persuasion and manipulation.
- Apply successful rhetorical strategies in your own writing.

Analyzing Rhetorical Effectiveness

Rhetorical strategies are techniques authors use to achieve their purposes. Common strategies include:

1. **Appeals to logic (logos):** Using evidence, data, and reasoned arguments
2. **Appeals to emotion (pathos):** Evoking emotional responses to motivate action
3. **Appeals to credibility (ethos):** Establishing the author's authority and trustworthiness
4. **Rhetorical questions:** Engaging readers by posing questions that prompt reflection
5. **Repetition and parallelism:** Using repeated structures for emphasis and memorability
6. **Vivid imagery:** Creating powerful mental pictures that engage readers' imaginations
7. **Storytelling:** Using narratives to illustrate points and create an emotional connection
8. **Metaphor and analogy:** Explaining complex concepts through

Example 4: Evaluating Rhetorical Strategies in a Speech

Let's analyze the rhetorical strategies in this excerpt from Nelson Mandela's inaugural address:

Excerpt from Mandela's Inaugural Address: "The time for the healing of the wounds has come. The moment to bridge the chasms that divide us has come. The time to build is upon us. We have, at last, achieved our political emancipation. We pledge ourselves to liberate all our people from the continuing bondage of poverty, deprivation, suffering, gender, and other discrimination.

We enter into a covenant that we shall build the society in which all South Africans, both black and white, will be able to walk tall, without any fear in their hearts, assured of their inalienable right to human dignity—a rainbow nation at peace with itself and the world."

Rhetorical strategies analysis:

1. **Parallelism and repetition:**
    - ◇ Repeated phrase structure: "The time... has come. The moment... has come."
    - ◇ Repeated pronoun "We" beginning multiple sentences
    - ◇ Effectiveness: Creates rhythm and emphasis, builds unity through inclusive "we"
2. **Metaphor and imagery:**
    - ◇ "healing of wounds" (nation as body)
    - ◇ "bridge the chasms" (division as physical gap)
    - ◇ "walk tall" (dignity as physical posture)
    - ◇ "rainbow nation" (diversity as natural beauty)
    - ◇ Effectiveness: Transforms abstract concepts into concrete, visual ideas
3. **Balanced contrasts:**
    - ◇ "black and white"
    - ◇ Past suffering vs. future hope
    - ◇ Effectiveness: Acknowledges difficult history while emphasizing unity

Example 5: Evaluating Rhetorical Effectiveness in Written Persuasion

Let's analyze the rhetorical strategies in this excerpt about climate change:

Excerpt from "Rising Waters, Rising Voices": "What would you do if the land where your ancestors are buried was disappearing beneath the waves? This is not a hypothetical question for Pacific Islanders—it is their daily reality. I met Teina on Kiribati's main atoll, where her family has lived for generations. At high tide, she showed me the coastal cemetery where saltwater now regularly washes over graves, including her grandfather's.

'When the land can no longer hold our dead,' she asked me, 'where will it find room for the living?'

We can debate policy details and implementation timelines, but we cannot debate physics. The laws of thermodynamics do not bend to political convenience. Each ton of carbon we emit melts more ice, raises more water, and brings the tide higher on shores around the world."

Rhetorical strategies analysis:

1. **Opening rhetorical question:**
   - ◇ Immediately engages readers by asking them to personally imagine the situation
2. **Narrative/storytelling:**
   - ◇ Personal account of meeting Teina transforms abstract climate data into human story
3. **Powerful quotation:**
   - ◇ Provides authentic voice from affected community in a poetic, memorable way
4. **Contrast:**
   - ◇ Juxtaposes debatable policies against non-negotiable physical laws
   - ◇ Effectiveness: Frames climate action as necessity rather than preference

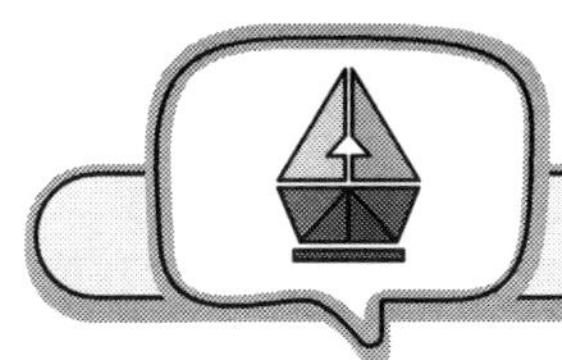

Rhetorical Strategy Analysis

Directions: Read the excerpts below and then answer the questions that follow.

Excerpt from President Barack Obama's Nobel Peace Prize Acceptance Speech (December 10, 2009)

"I face the world as it is, and cannot stand idle in the face of threats to the American people. For make no mistake: evil does exist in the world. A non-violent movement could not have halted Hitler's armies. Negotiations cannot convince al Qaeda's leaders to lay down their arms. To say that force may sometimes be necessary is not a call to cynicism—it is a recognition of history; the imperfections of man and the limits of reason."

"So part of our challenge is reconciling these two seemingly irreconcilable truths—that war is sometimes necessary, and war at some level is an expression of human folly."

Question 1: Which rhetorical strategy does President Obama employ in the excerpt to justify the potential necessity of force in international affairs?

A. Appeal to Emotion (Pathos): By invoking the existence of evil and referencing historical atrocities, Obama elicits an emotional response to justify the use of force.

B. Appeal to Logic (Logos): Obama presents logical arguments, citing historical examples where non-violence failed, to rationalize the necessity of force.

C. Ethical Appeal (Ethos): He establishes his credibility by acknowledging the moral complexities leaders face, thereby justifying his stance on the use of force.

D. Repetition: Obama repeats key phrases to emphasize the inevitability of conflict and the need for preparedness.

Question 2: What is the primary rhetorical effect of Obama juxtaposing the ideas that war is both 'necessary' and 'an expression of human folly'?

A. to illustrate the inevitability of armed conflict in global politics

B. to diminish the moral weight of military decisions

C. to highlight the moral and philosophical tension involved in the use of force

D. to criticize historical leaders for embracing war too easily

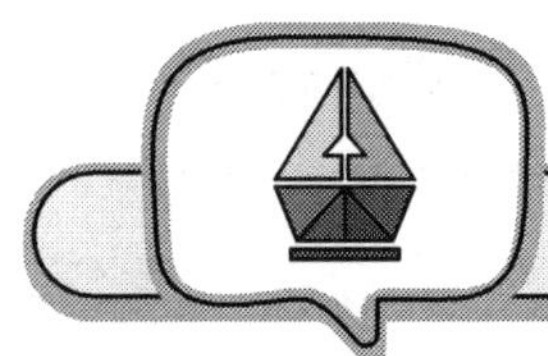

Week 5 • Practice Activity 3

Question 3: Which phrase from the excerpt best signals Obama's implicit purpose to promote ethical reflection on global leadership?

A. "evil does exist in the world"

B. "negotiations cannot convince al Qaeda's leaders"

C. "a recognition of history"

D. "the imperfections of man and the limits of reason"

Note:

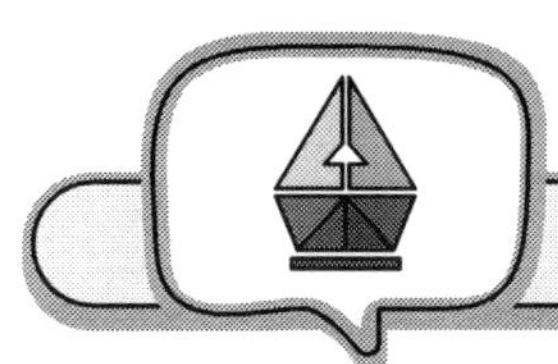

Week 5 • Final Reflection Questions

Directions: Take a few minutes to think about the lessons from this week, and then answer the questions below.

Question 1: How does recognizing both explicit and implicit authorial purpose help you read more critically, especially in persuasive or emotionally charged texts?

Question 2: Why is it important to consider an author's cultural or historical context when analyzing their purpose? How might ignoring context lead to misinterpretation or bias?

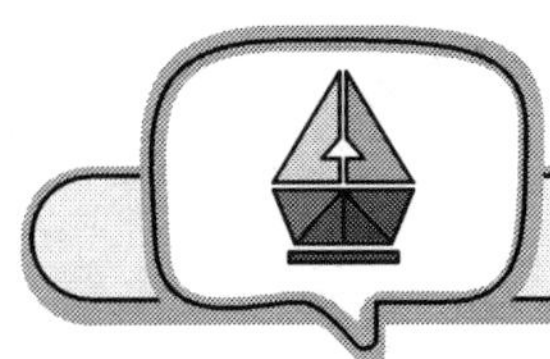

Awesome! Next week, we will begin tackling literary texts.

Final Thought

Understanding an author's purpose transforms you from a passive reader into an active, critical thinker. When you recognize why someone writes—whether to inform, persuade, entertain, or some combination—you gain valuable insight into how to interpret their message. You've learned to identify both explicit and implicit purposes, analyze how these purposes shape content and organization, and evaluate how effectively authors achieve their goals with specific audiences. These skills are essential not just for academic success but for navigating our information-rich world. Advertisements, news articles, political speeches, and social media posts all have purposes that may not be immediately obvious. By approaching texts with the analytical tools you've developed this week, you'll be better equipped to recognize when someone is trying to inform you, persuade you, or perhaps even manipulate you. This awareness makes you a more discerning reader, a more critical consumer of information, and ultimately, a more effective communicator yourself.

ANSWER
KEY
ARGOPREP

Answer Sheets

To see the answer key to the entire workbook, you can easily download the answer key from our website!

*Due to the high request from parents and teachers, we have removed the answer key from the workbook so you do not need to rip out the answer key while students work on the workbook.

To watch free video explanations go to: **argoprep.com/ela10book1**

OR scan the QR Code:

Place your mouse over the workbook you have, and you will see the "Download Answers" button.

For detailed video instructions on how to access the "Answer Sheets," please scan this QR code.